The Time is Now

The Time is Now

BY

JULIE ROWE

spring creek
BOOK COMPANY
Provo, Utah

ISBN: 978-0-9960974-1-3
e. 1

Published by:
Spring Creek Book Company
P.O. Box 50355
Provo, Utah 84605-0355

www.springcreekbooks.com

Cover Image © istockphoto.com/Andrew_Mayovskyy
Cover design © Spring Creek Book Company

Printed in the United States of America

TABLE OF CONTENTS

ACKNOWLEDGMENTS VII

CHAPTER ONE.. I
The Lord's Prophets Have Spoken

CHAPTER TWO 17
The Hastening of the Work

CHAPTER THREE 27
The Power of Family History and Temple Work

CHAPTER FOUR 32
Don't Delay Getting Your Life in Order

CHAPTER FIVE.. 43
Spiritual Preparations Before the Gathering

CHAPTER SIX 50
Temporal Preparations Before the Gathering

CHAPTER SEVEN 65
Church Leaders Will Prepare the Saints

CHAPTER EIGHT 71
The Prophet's Invitation to Gather

CHAPTER NINE 80
Daily Life in the Three Types of Camps

CHAPTER TEN 89
Natural Disasters Across the Earth

CHAPTER ELEVEN 103
Plagues and Sicknesses

CHAPTER TWELVE.................................... 111
The U.S. Government Implements Martial Law

CHAPTER THIRTEEN 115
Foreign Troops Arrive on U.S. Soil

CHAPTER FOURTEEN 120
The Saints Gather into Larger Groups

CHAPTER FIFTEEN 124
The Elders of Israel Defend Their Liberty

CHAPTER SIXTEEN.................................. 128
Life in New Jerusalem

 CHAPTER SEVENTEEN 136
The Second Coming of the Savior

APPENDIX 147
The Emotion Code and The Body Code

ABOUT THE AUTHOR............................. 157

ACKNOWLEDGMENTS

First and foremost I would like to thank our loving Father in Heaven for the blessing and opportunity He has given me to share this message. I am grateful for the many tender mercies and miracles which have occurred in my life, particularly over the past several weeks as I have worked on writing this second book. I am grateful for divine intervention which has made it possible, and for the knowledge the Lord has given me. I hope this book, as well as my first book, *A Greater Tomorrow*, is of benefit to others.

I would like to thank my husband and children for their loving patience, sacrifices and willingness to support me in sharing this message. It is no easy thing having your wife and mother busy writing one book, let alone two books within a period of less than six months. Additionally, I am grateful for their willingness to support me as I travel to speak in various locations. I could not do what I need to do without their help, support and encouragement.

I am grateful for so many good people who have sent me positive and uplifting messages of gratitude and encouragement. Thank you for your kindness and for your faith and testimonies. Your messages have strengthened me and have continued to buoy me up despite the opposition.

I am also very grateful to and for Chad Daybell, and his sweet wife Tammy. They are incredible people and I am forever thankful for the blessing I have had to work with them on this book. They are both inspired individuals and it has been an absolute pleasure working with them. I am grateful for Tammy and her continued support of Chad as he has spent many hours working on these two books. I know it has been a great sacrifice for Chad's family as he has dedicated so much time and energy to making sure both *A Greater Tomorrow* and *The Time is Now* could be published in a timely manner.

Tammy and Chad have done a marvelous job on both book covers, which were truly inspired. I have learned so much from working with Chad. I am eternally grateful for his testimony, faith, example, and encouragement in helping me to accomplish this work. He is a talented man, but one of the qualities I respect most about him is his humble obedience and willingness to listen to and follow the Spirit. Writing these two books has been hard work, but it has been worth it. The Lord could not have chosen two better people to help me in this endeavor. Thank you so much, Chad and Tammy, for all you have done and for all that you are. Love you guys!

CHAPTER ONE

⁂

The Lord's Prophets Have Spoken

I am grateful for the blessing and opportunity to write this second book, and share with others more of my experiences. For those who have not yet read my first book, *A Greater Tomorrow*, I recommend reading it first, if possible. The first book gives the reader a basic understanding of what I experienced during my Near Death Experience in 2004, and it provides a foundation for this second book.

Although I have written this book to be read and understood as a stand-alone work of its own, it is written as a follow-up to the first book. My hope is that between the two books, I have been able to clearly, concisely, and accurately share my experiences with others so they may benefit from what I have written.

This book serves several purposes. It provides an additional witness of our Savior Jesus Christ, and of Heavenly Father's Eternal Plan of Happiness for each of His children. It also gives an additional voice of warning, with the hope that what I share will help others prepare temporally and spiritually for the days ahead. My intention was to share portions of what I have been shown and taught concerning events of the last days and what will soon come to pass on the earth.

I do not claim any kind of stewardship over anyone other than my own family. What I share is based on my own limited knowledge and understanding of what has been given to me from our very loving Father in Heaven to help me and my family. This knowledge is also to help me fulfill the assignment I have been given by the Lord to spread His gospel, testify of eternal truths, and encourage others to seek answers to their own questions.

I am simply sharing a portion of my experience, and I do so with the intention of helping, encouraging, uplifting, and edifying anyone who chooses to read my words.

I pray that what I share in this book will motivate others to seek further light and knowledge of their own, and that what I write will resonate with those who need to hear the message. I pray that those who learn about my experience will take what I share and use it to help others.

I pray that we may each learn how to discern the Spirit, and in turn be able to understand the important truths the Lord would have us know individually and collectively.

I know that as we each do our part to further the Lord's work, we may each come to a greater understanding of who we are and what it is that we are meant to accomplish. I pray that I may be a simple instrument in the Lord's hands to bring others into the fold and reach out to those who may be lost, confused, worried, or otherwise afflicted.

As I briefly explained in my first book, in September of 2004 I had what some would call "A Near Death Experience." I was shown many places and people in the Spirit World. Since I have already written about that event in *A Greater Tomorrow*, I will not repeat those details here.

In the first book I also shared information about key historical events. I do not have permission from the Lord to share additional details regarding the past, other than to give a few general historical summaries. As I go forward in writing this second book

I have been instructed to focus on those things which will help us prepare for the future. My intent is to help any of God's children awaken to the realities of our day, and to do what I can to serve the Lord in doing my small part in building His Kingdom here upon the earth.

Having said that, I need to emphasize that in no way do I officially represent The Church of Jesus Christ of Latter-day Saints, and I do not speak for the leaders of the Church. I fully sustain each Prophet and Apostle of the LDS Church, and I know without a doubt that our current leaders hold the priesthood keys to this dispensation, which is the fullness of times.

President Thomas S. Monson is a Prophet of God. He leads and guides the Lord's Church upon the earth at this time. The First Presidency of the Church and members of the Quorum of the Twelve Apostles have been called and set apart by God as Prophets, Seers and Revelators. They have been called as Special Witnesses of Jesus Christ. I sustain them in their callings and know they are men of God who seek to do His will in all things.

A House of Order

The Lord's house is a house of order. We have each been foreordained to fulfill specific missions in this life. The Lord has foreordained and called our prophets and apostles, and under His direction, they have and are fulfilling His purposes. It is they who hold the keys of stewardship for the Church and the Lord's Kingdom here upon the earth.

When looking for guidance and direction, we need to first turn to the Lord, and then also to our Church leaders who have been placed in positions of authority for our safety and well-being. We need to listen to and obey the counsel of our Prophets, Seers, and Revelators. They have been given the power and authority to act in God's name.

We must learn and know for ourselves what it is the Lord would have us do to protect ourselves and our families from the difficult days that are upon us. We must do all within our power to withstand the adversary. The time is now for us to take a stand in defense of righteousness and to stand in holy places.

A Remarkable Conference Session

The Sunday morning session of the October 2014 General Conference began with three remarkable talks that emphasized the importance of following the living prophet.

President Henry B. Eyring, First Counselor in the First Presidency, began the session by speaking about the importance of the prophet in our daily lives.

President Eyring said, "Don't take lightly the feeling you get of love for the prophet of God. Wherever I go in the Church, whoever the prophet is at the time, members will ask, 'When you get back to Church headquarters, will you please tell the prophet how much we love him?'

"That is far more than hero worship or the feelings we sometimes have of admiring heroic figures. It is a gift from God. With it you will receive more easily the gift of confirming revelation when he speaks in his office as the Lord's prophet. The love you feel is the love the Lord has for whomever is His spokesman.

"That is not easy to feel continually because the Lord often asks His prophets to give counsel that is hard for people to accept. The enemy of our souls will try to lead us to take offense and to doubt the prophet's calling from God." (*Ensign*, "Continuing Revelation," November 2014)

President Eyring was followed by Elder Russell M. Nelson, who said, "Often we sing, 'We Thank Thee, O God, for a Prophet.' Do you and I really understand what that means? Imagine the privilege the Lord has given us of sustaining His prophet, whose counsel will be untainted, unvarnished, unmotivated by any personal aspiration and utterly true!"

He later added, "The Church today has been organized by the Lord Himself. He has put in place a remarkable system of governance that provides redundancy and backup. That system provides for prophetic leadership even when the inevitable illness and incapacities may come with advancing age. Counterbalances and safeguards abound so that no one man can ever lead the Church astray. Senior leaders are constantly being tutored such that one day they are ready to sit in the highest councils. They learn how to hear the voice of the Lord through the whisperings of the Spirit." (*Ensign*, "Sustaining the Prophets," November 2014)

Then Sister Carol F. McConkie, First Counselor in the Young Women General Presidency, expressed her gratitude to be part of a church with living apostles and prophets led by Jesus Christ.

"In a world threatened by famine of righteousness and spiritual starvation, we have been commanded to sustain the prophet. As we give heed to, uphold and affirm prophetic word, we witness that we have the faith to humbly submit to the will, the wisdom and the timing of the Lord."

Sister McConkie added, "We heed prophetic word even when it may seem unreasonable, inconvenient and uncomfortable. According to the world's standards, following the prophet may be unpopular, politically incorrect or socially unacceptable. But following the prophet is always right." (*Ensign*, "Live According to the Words of the Prophets," November 2014)

I am grateful for these timely words from our inspired Church leaders. Our obedience to the counsel the prophets have given and will yet give, will soon be a matter of life and death, both temporally and spiritually. We cannot afford to be complacent or to discard their counsel. We cannot afford to be idle and ignore that which the Lord has commanded us to do. Time is short. The time to prepare is now.

We Each Have a Specified Plan

Father in Heaven has a specified plan for each of us. In the pre-mortal world, we had agency, much like we do today. We took part in the Grand Councils in Heaven, and we chose to come to earth to receive the bodies we have been given. We chose to come to earth at this time, and we took part in planning many of the experiences we would have while in this mortal existence.

There is a purpose in all things as they pertain to our eternal welfare and the Lord's plan for us. We cannot forget this. We must always remember that there is reason and purpose in all things, even when we do not know or understand what that may be.

I was clearly shown and taught that all things, even the very things that cause us our greatest pain and suffering—and even those experiences which test us to the very core—are all for our learning and good. Our experiences while here in mortality are meant to teach, edify, refine, and purify us. It is because of these trials, not just in spite of them, that we are able to become who and what we are meant to become and who the Lord knows we truly are.

I testify of this truth. I know that with God, all things are possible. We truly can do all things through Christ. No matter the opposition and no matter how impossible it may seem, we can do anything we set our minds to when we have pure intent and complete trust and faith in God.

Through the very real tender mercies of our loving Father in Heaven, we can change. We can learn, grow, and develop. We can overcome any adversity we may face as we seek to do His will, rather than our own.

We must trust in Him. We must use our agency to seek that which is of the light. We must put aside the things of this world and turn our hearts and minds to that which truly matters: God, faith, family, and freedom.

The Prophets Have Spoken Plainly

It has come to my attention that there are some among us who either do not know or do not believe that the Lord's servants have spoken plainly concerning the state of affairs in our nation and across the world. There are some who are not aware of the words of our modern day prophets and apostles. There are some who do not know or understand the importance of following the Prophet and heeding his counsel.

There are others who, although aware, are choosing not to follow the counsel we have been given. There are those among us who are choosing not to listen and obey. There are some who do not know where to find these truths, and consequently are being tossed to and fro by the whirlwinds of the world.

These are some of the reasons I will share just a small portion of what the Lord has given us through the mouths of His modern day prophets and apostles. I cannot begin to quote every word that has been given concerning the need to prepare temporally and spiritually, but I will share a few applicable messages.

I do so in an effort to express in all sincerity the need each of us has to study these things out on our own, and to increase our knowledge and understanding of the many words of warning we are continually being given by the Lord.

It is up to us to open our hearts and minds to the messages that are available through the promptings of the Holy Spirit. It is up to us to listen and obey once we have been given further light and knowledge. It is up to us to learn to recognize when and how the Spirit speaks to us.

We can know the truth of all things through the power of the Holy Ghost. The Spirit speaks to us individually in many different ways, in the manner the Lord knows we are able to best receive it. Each of us has been endowed with specific gifts given to us by the Lord.

Personal revelation comes to us individually as we do our part to repent of those things which are not in keeping with the Lord's ways. It comes to us as we study, ponder, and pray about those things we seek to know and understand. As we are obedient to the Lord's commandments and do all we can to apply the Atonement in our lives, we will learn to feel and then act on the promptings we are given.

Doing Our Part

For us to become the beneficiaries of personal revelation, we need to do our part. We need to act upon the promptings we are given and to remain steadfast in our determination to listen and obey, even when we do not have total clarity, understanding, or knowledge as to what or why we have been given a directive. When we act on our faith and are obedient to the Lord's commands, we show our Father in Heaven that we are trustworthy.

The more we trust the Lord and follow the guidance of the Holy Spirit, the more the Lord trusts us. When we show Him that we are willing to listen and obey in all things, no matter the sacrifice, then the Lord trusts us with more. He is waiting and willing to give us all He has. However, He will not give us more than we can handle. This pertains not only to the trials we endure, but also to the amount of light and knowledge He bestows upon us.

God loves us so much that He will not tell us more than we need to know at any given time. He will only reveal what we need to know, when we need to know it, as He sees fit. He does not withhold information as a means of control or punishment. He refrains from telling us certain things at certain times in our lives because He knows all and He knows what is in our best interest and what will be for our greatest good.

Father in Heaven wants us to succeed. He believes in us. He

knows the end from the beginning. He knows who we are and what we can become. He knows what is best for us and what we need to learn to accomplish the ultimate goal, which is to return to live with Him and receive our exaltation.

Agency is Essential

The Lord is bound by the eternal laws of the universe. Agency is an eternal principle. No matter the circumstance, Father in Heaven will never take away our agency. He has and always will protect our freedom to choose and act for ourselves.

God knows that agency is essential to the Great Plan of Happiness. He will do all in His power to positively influence, guide and direct our actions so that we may benefit from the blessings made available to us. But ultimately the choice is ours to choose for ourselves the path we will take and the life we will live. The Lord has given us Prophets, Apostles, the scriptures, and the Holy Spirit to be our guide. It is up to us to choose whether or not we will listen and obey.

Warnings from the Modern Prophets

For thousands of years we have been warned again and again about the need to prepare for the Day of the Lord. We have been told repeatedly that Christ will come again. Yet a common question I have received concerning my first book is that people wonder why the prophets have been "silent" on such matters.

The fact is the prophets and apostles have preached for years concerning the events of the Last Days, and they have warned us repeatedly to be temporally and spiritually prepared.

I will share several quotes throughout the book, but I will conclude this chapter by sharing a prophetic statement from each of the 16 prophets who have led the LDS Church since it was established in 1830. Their messages are clear and consistent concerning the troubling fate of the United States if the citizens fail to repent. Their words are sobering. Let us take heed.

Joseph Smith: I saw men hunting the lives of their own sons, and brother murdering brother, women killing their own daughters, and daughters seeking the lives of their mothers. I saw armies arrayed against armies. I saw blood, desolation, fires. The Son of Man has said that the mother shall be against the daughter, and the daughter against the mother. These things are at our doors. They will follow the Saints of God from city to city. (*History of the Church*, 3:391)

Brigham Young: Do you think there is calamity abroad now among the people? Not much. All we have yet heard and all we have experienced is scarcely a preface to the sermon that is going to be preached.

When the testimony of the Elders ceases to be given, and the Lord says to them, "Come home; I will now preach my own sermons to the nations of the earth," all you now know can scarcely be called a preface to the sermon that will be preached with fire and sword, tempests, earthquakes, hail, rain, thunders and lightnings, and fearful destruction.

What matters the destruction of a few railway cars? You will hear of magnificent cities, now idolized by the people, sinking in the earth, entombing the inhabitants. The sea will heave itself beyond its bounds, engulfing mighty cities. Famine will spread over the nations, and nation will rise up against nation, kingdom against kingdom, and states against states, in our own country and in foreign lands; and they will destroy each other, caring not for the blood and lives of their neighbors, of their families, or for their own lives. (*Journal of Discourses*, Vol. 8:123)

John Taylor: Were we surprised when the last terrible war (the Civil War) took place here in the United States? No. Good Latter-day Saints were not, for they had been told about it. Joseph Smith had told them where it would start in South Carolina. But I tell you today the end is not yet. You will see worse things than that, for God will lay his hand upon this nation, and they will feel it more terribly than even they have done before.

There will be more bloodshed, more ruin, more devastation than ever they have seen before. Write it down! You will see it come to pass; it is only just starting in. And would you feel to rejoice? No; I would feel sorry.

I knew very well myself when this last war was commencing and could have wept and did weep, over this nation; but there is yet to come a sound of war, trouble and distress, in which brother will be arrayed against brother, father against son, son against father, a scene of desolation and destruction that will permeate our land until it will be a vexation to hear the report thereof. (*Journal of Discourses,* Vol. 20:318)

Wilford Woodruff: The Lord is not going to disappoint either Babylon or Zion, with regard to famine, pestilence, earthquake or storms. He is not going to disappoint anybody with regard to any of these things, they are at the doors. Lay up your wheat and other provisions against a day of need, for the day will come when they will be wanted, make no mistake about it. We shall want bread, and the Gentiles will want bread, and if we are wise we shall have something to feed them and ourselves when famine comes. (*Journal of Discourses,* Vol. 18:121)

Lorenzo Snow: How many now here, are ready—having oil in their vessels, and lamps trimmed, and prepared for coming events? I am not sorry, nor do I regret on account of the near approach of these fiery ordeals; the Church, no doubt, needs purifying—

we have hypocrites among us—milk-and-water Saints—those professing to be Saints, but doing nothing to render themselves worthy of membership; and too many of us have been pursuing worldly gains, rather than spiritual improvements—have not sought the things of God with that earnestness which becomes our profession. Trials and afflictions will cause our hearts to turn towards our Father who has so marvelously wrought out our redemption and deliverance from Babylon. (*Journal of Discourses,* Vol. 6:367-68)

Joseph F. Smith: We know that the spirit of strife and contention exists to an alarming extent among the people of the world. Why does it exist? Because they are not one with God, nor with Christ. They have not entered into the true fold, and the result is they do not possess the spirit of the true Shepherd sufficiently to govern and control their acts and the ways of peace and righteousness.

Thus they contend and strive one against another, and at last nation rises up against nation in fulfillment of the predictions of the prophets of God that war should be poured out upon all nations. (*Conference Report,* October 1914, p. 8)

Heber J. Grant: I believe that nearly all of the hardships of a majority of the people would disappear if they were willing to forego the habit of wearing silk stockings, so to speak, and get back to the ordinary manner of dressing in a rather quiet, unassuming way; stay away from about nine-tenths of the picture shows that they attend; and return to the ways of thrift and economy that I have heard preached from this stand from the days of President Brigham Young until today. (*Conference Report,* April 1923, p.8)

George Albert Smith: We live in a great and wonderful age. The glory of this century is beyond that of any other century; but

I feel that we are in just as great danger as were those who lived in the days of Noah, or those who lived in the days of Nephi upon this great western land.

We are in as great danger as any nation that has ever lived, because God has given us more than any other nation, and if in arrogance and in pride we turn aside from the Father of us all, and in our carelessness and indifference towards sacred things we spend our lives for the things of this world, it will not be very long until the chastening hand of an all-wise Father may come upon us as a nation, and we be counted as the nations of the past, among those that have withered away. (*Conference Report*, October 1928, p. 94)

David O. McKay: Approximately only a quarter century ago, the world listened to the clanging of arms of nations fighting in a world-wide war that was supposed to end war forever. Up to that time it was the bloodiest war in history. Again, misguided leaders of nations, worshipping the god of materialism, have brought on World War II, and unless the nations avoid the evil things which caused this war, there will be a World War III even more destructive and more terrible than the present murderous conflict. (*Improvement Era*, 47:657, given in 1944)

Joseph Fielding Smith: We may safely say that today the anger of the Lord is kindled against this generation for its wickedness, and the earth groans under the weight of iniquity which is practiced upon its face. The Almighty has not forgotten his promise made to Enoch, and the day is soon at hand when the earth again will be cleansed of all iniquity and shall rest for a thousand years. (Moses 7:60-61)

It is very displeasing to some self-righteous souls to have anyone speak of these things and say that punishment by war, pestilence, famine, and the disturbance of the elements, is coming upon mankind by decree of a just God, because of the transgressions of his holy laws. Nevertheless this happens to be the case, for the Lord has declared it. His anger is kindled against the abominations and sins of the world. (*Church News*, August 2, 1941, p. 1)

Harold B. Lee: The spirit of gathering has been with the Church from the days of that restoration. Those who are of the blood of Israel have a righteous desire after they are baptized, to gather together with the body of the Saints at the designated place. This, we have come to recognize, is but the breath of God upon those who are converted, turning them to the promises made to their fathers.

The designation of gathering places is qualified in another revelation by the Lord. After designating certain places in that day where the Saints were to gather, the Lord said: "Until the day cometh when there is found no more room for them; and then I have other places which I will appoint unto them" (D&C 101:21).

Thus, the Lord has placed the responsibility for directing the work of gathering in the hands of the leaders of the Church, to whom he will reveal his will where and when such gatherings would take place in the future.

It would be well, before the frightening events concerning the fulfilment of all God's promises and predictions are upon us, that the Saints in every land prepare themselves and look forward to the instruction that shall come to them from the First Presidency of this Church as to where they shall be gathered and not be disturbed in their feelings until such instruction is given to them as it is revealed by the Lord to the proper authority. (*The Teachings of Harold B. Lee*, p. 410)

Spencer W. Kimball: We continue on in our godlessness. While the iron curtains rise and thicken, we eat, drink, and make merry. While armies are marshaled and march and drill, and officers teach men how to kill, we continue to drink and carouse as usual. While bombs are detonated and tested, and fallout settles on the already sick world, we continue in idolatry and adultery. While corridors are threatened and concessions are made, we live riotously and divorce and marry in cycles like the seasons. While leaders quarrel, and editors write, and authorities analyze and prognosticate, we break the Sabbath as though no command had ever been given. While enemies filter into our nation to subvert us and intimidate us and soften us, we continue with our destructive thinking: "It can't happen here."

Will we ever turn wholly to God? Fear envelops the world which could be at ease and peace. In God is protection, safety, peace. He has said, "I will fight your battles" (D&C 105:14). But his commitment is on condition of our faithfulness. (*The Teachings of Spencer W. Kimball*, p. 416)

Ezra Taft Benson: There is a real sifting going on in the Church, and it is going to become more pronounced with the passing of time. It will sift the wheat from the tares, because we face some difficult days, the like of which we have never experienced in our lives. And those days are going to require faith and testimony and family unity, the like of which we have never had. (*The Teachings of Ezra Taft Benson*, p. 107)

Howard W. Hunter: I promise you tonight in the name of the Lord whose servant I am that God will always protect and care for his people. We will have our difficulties the way every generation and people have had difficulties. Your life as a young college student or working person in the 1990s is no different than any young person's life has been in any age of time. But with the gospel of Jesus Christ you have every hope and promise and reassurance. The Lord has power over his Saints and will always prepare places of peace, defense, and safety for his people. When we have faith in God we can hope for a better world—for us personally and for all mankind. (*The Teachings of Howard W. Hunter*, p. 201)

Gordon B. Hinckley: I urge you, brethren, to look to the condition of your finances. I urge you to be modest in your expenditures; discipline yourselves in your purchases to avoid debt to the extent possible. Pay off debt as quickly as you can, and free yourselves from bondage.

This is a part of the temporal gospel in which we believe. May the Lord bless you, my beloved brethren, to set your houses in order. If you have paid your debts, if you have a reserve, even though it be small, then should storms howl about your head, you will have shelter for your wives and children and peace in your hearts. (*Conference Report*, October 1998)

Thomas S. Monson: Are we prepared for the emergencies in our lives? Are our skills perfected? Do we live providently? Do we have our reserve supply on hand? Are we obedient to the commandments of God? Are we responsive to the teachings of the prophets? Are we prepared to give of our substance to the poor, the needy? Are we square with the Lord? We live in turbulent times. Often the future is unknown; therefore, it behooves us to prepare for uncertainties. When the time for decision arrives, the time for preparation is past. (*Ensign*, September 2014, p.5)

CHAPTER TWO

———— ❧ ————

The Hastening of the Work

The Lord is hastening His work in these latter days. As prophesied in scripture, the great work of bringing souls unto Christ has begun and will continue to increase significantly prior to the Second Coming. This applies not only to the tremendous missionary effort here on the earth, but also to that which has been done and continues to occur in the Spirit World.

Missionary work has always been part of God's plan for His children. It was part of our experience in the premortal world. It is part of God's plan here upon the earth now, and it is part of His eternal plan for those who return to the Spirit World after mortality. It will also continue after the Second Coming and take place throughout the Millennium.

It is through missionary work that we help to bring about God's eternal purposes for His children. It is how we learn about and receive the necessary saving ordinances which are obtained through baptism and temple attendance.

The books of Daniel, Joel, Isaiah, Revelation, and many other scriptures prophesy that prior to the Savior's return there will be a hastening of the work in many ways. In addition to a growth in missionary efforts, temple work and Family History work will increase. Additional light and knowledge will be felt among the people. Many who have been lost will be found.

During my journey to the Spirit World, I was shown a great deal about the history of the earth. I was shown some of the significant events that led to the great apostasy which is described in the book of Amos in the Old Testament. God knew there would be an apostasy, and He planned accordingly.

The Lord said: "Behold, the days come...that I will send a famine in the land, not a famine of bread, nor a thirst for water, but of hearing the words of the Lord:

"And (people) shall wander from sea to sea, and from the north even to the east, they shall run to and fro to seek the word of the Lord, and shall not find it." (Amos 8: 11-12)

Scenes of Apostasy

I was shown scenes depicting this very thing, with thousands of people wandering to and fro, looking for truth and struggling to find answers to life's great mysteries. I saw kings, queens, presidents and magistrates ruling throughout the centuries in darkness and fear. I witnessed leaders of armies and nations traveling great distances in search of knowledge and power.

I saw prophets traveling about and testifying to various people, encountering many whose eyes were blinded and whose hearts were cold and unreceptive to the messages of the Gospel. I witnessed the persecution, torture and bloodshed of many of the righteous followers of Christ. I saw some of the confusion and darkness that covered the land.

I was shown scenes from the lives of the Twelve Apostles whom Christ had called and set apart to become "fishers of men." I witnessed the events that led to the end of some of their mortal ministries. I witnessed the destruction of towns, villages and peoples of all nations and of varying backgrounds.

It was horrific. It was humbling. It was overwhelming. My heart was broken as I witnessed some of the wicked acts and severe atrocities that have taken place on this planet. I sobbed as I witnessed these events and more. At times I had to close my eyes and turn my head because I could not bear to see it.

It was at these moments that the Spirit calmed my soul and brought peace to my troubled heart. It was during these experiences that I came to a full and complete knowledge and understanding of God's plan for His children. It was during these experiences that I came to more fully comprehend that God truly does in fact have a divine plan for each of His children.

It was made very clear to me that God knew there would be an apostasy, and because of this, He inspired the prophets and apostles to write about the last days and the hastening of the work that would happen prior to the Second Coming. He had them testify of the things that He had shown them in dreams and visions. God specifically foreordained and called upon the Apostle John to write about the things he had been shown pertaining to the last days and the Second Coming of the Lord. Some of John's prophecies are recorded in the Book of Revelation.

Through the scriptures, we learn about God's plan for the Restoration of the Gospel of Jesus Christ. We learn that the Lord foreordained many great men and women to bring about the immense work of saving souls and redeeming the dead. We learn that prior to Christ's return, "the hearts of the children will turn to their fathers," just as the prophet Elijah taught.

Missionary Efforts to Increase

Missionary work has always been the focus of the Church. The message of hastening the work has increased the past few years, particularly after President Monson announced the lowering of the ages when missionaries could begin their service. I was shown that the Church's formal missionary efforts will continue and even increase significantly in the near future.

Elder D. Todd Christofferson of the Quorum of the Twelve Apostles has said, "For me, the missionary purpose captures the majesty of the work and glory of God (see Moses 1:39). What endeavor is more magnificent than bringing the children of God to ultimate salvation through the grace of their Redeemer, the Lord Jesus Christ? Remember that our missionary purpose is not only to warn others but also to save them, not only to teach but also to baptize, not only to bring others unto Christ but also to make them steadfast in Christ to the end.

"Our invitation to the world is to come unto Christ. Coming unto Christ is an abbreviation, a way of describing in three words the plan of salvation. It means to obtain the fruits of His Atonement and Resurrection—ultimately eternal life. Eternal life depends on the exercise of our moral agency, but it is possible only through the grace of Jesus Christ. To come unto Him means to do what is required to lay hold upon that grace—the pardoning, sanctifying, transforming, redeeming power of His infinite, atoning sacrifice.

"As we share testimony of the gospel by the Spirit, those who are willing to hear will receive sufficient witness to begin to have faith in Jesus Christ and His Atonement. That faith will give them the will to repent." (*Ensign*, August 2014, p. 36-38)

Technology Will Help Spread the Gospel

The gospel is being spread in many ways. Elder David A. Bednar of the Quorum of the Twelve Apostles gave a masterful presentation at the 2014 BYU Education Week in regard to how technology will help spread the gospel to every corner of the earth. He said, "What has been accomplished thus far in this dispensation communicating gospel messages through social media channels is a good beginning—but only a small trickle. I now extend to you the invitation to help transform the trickle into a flood. Beginning at this place on this day, I exhort you to sweep the earth with messages filled with righteousness and truth—messages that are authentic, edifying, and praiseworthy—and literally to sweep the earth as with a flood." (*Church News*, August 24, 2104, p. 5)

This accelerated burst of missionary work is a merciful and miraculous effort by the Lord to save as many of His children as will listen to the gospel message. Many Church members are under the impression that this growth will continue exponentially until the Second Coming, but the scriptures and the words of the prophets indicate that is not the case.

The Missionaries Will Be Called Home

There will come a time when our missionaries who are serving abroad will be called home, and the Church will no longer send missionaries out into the mission field like we do today. The conditions of the world will be such that traditional methods of missionary work will cease for a time, although some will be called upon to stay in their respective areas and assist with the work there.

Why would this happen when things are going so well? It will be caused by the wickedness of the world.

Elder Orson Pratt taught: "When God has called out the righteous, when the warning voice has been sufficiently proclaimed among the Gentile nations, and the Lord says, 'It is enough,' he will also say to his servants—'O, ye, my servants, come home, come out from the midst of these Gentile nations, where you have labored and borne testimony for so long a period; come out from among them, for they are not worthy; they do not receive the message that I have sent forth, they do not repent of their sins, come out from their midst, their times are fulfilled. Seal up the testimony among them and bind up the law.'" (*Journal of Discourses*, Vol. 18:64, given on July 25, 1875)

Elder Heber C. Kimball taught the Saints, "The judgments of God will be poured out upon the wicked to the extent that our elders from far and near will be called home. Or, in other words, the gospel will be taken from the Gentiles and later on be carried to the Jews." (*Deseret News*, May 23, 1931, p.3, originally given in May 1868)

I also refer again to the statement from President Brigham Young that I quoted in Chapter One, where he testified that the day will come when the Lord will say, "Come home; I will now preach my own sermons to the nations of the earth."

Sharing the Gospel with All the World

This has led some people to ask me, "How is it possible that the Lord would gather his children to Places of Refuge in preparation for the Lord's Second Coming, when there are still so many countries we have yet to enter into and preach the gospel?"

They have struggled to understand the timing of things and how these scriptures will come to pass. That is understandable, since we have been told by prophets and the scriptures that the gospel must go to all the world. We have yet to send formal missionaries into places like Yemen, Iran, North Korea or China. There are many millions of people who have still not been taught the fullness of the gospel of Jesus Christ.

Let me explain a bit. The gospel of Jesus Christ has in fact been introduced in each of these countries as well as others, although not necessarily in the traditional sense as far as the Church sending full-time missionaries into every land. For example, in the case of China, for more than 1,000 years the gospel of Jesus Christ has spread its influence across the country. Although the majority of those in China have not been taught the fullness of the gospel, many have been taught of Christ. Over the years, thousands of Christians have been severely persecuted for their religious beliefs.

Many have been martyred for their testimonies of Christ.

I was shown vivid examples of some of the lives of Chinese Christians. I was specifically shown some of the history of that nation, and the missionary efforts that have been in place for years. It was made very clear to me that the gospel is slowly spreading, and that the day will come when our missionaries will travel from afar to preach of the Restored Gospel of Jesus Christ.

The same can be said for every nation. The scriptures teach us that the gospel will be preached throughout the world to every tongue and people. They teach us that this will happen before the Second Coming of the Lord. They do not tell us how or even exactly when that will happen. It is my understanding that through the use of modern technology, specifically the internet, the gospel is now being taught in almost every nation.

The 144,000

This means that formal missionary work will mostly cease during the upcoming times of tribulation and war. This could last for several years. However, there will come a point in time when the Lord will once again send out His missionary force—a unique group of 144,000 Saints.

In Doctrine and Covenants 77:11, the Lord tells Joseph Smith specifically about their special mission.

"11 Q. What are we to understand by sealing the one hundred and forty-four thousand, out of all the tribes of Israel—twelve thousand out of every tribe?

"A. We are to understand that those who are sealed are high priests, ordained unto the holy order of God, to administer the everlasting gospel; for they are they who are ordained out of every nation, kindred, tongue, and people, by the angels to whom is given power over the nations of the earth, to bring as many as will come to the church of the Firstborn."

As the scripture explains, these 144,000 missionaries will consist of 12,000 High Priests (and in some cases their wives), from each of the Twelve Tribes of Israel. They have been foreordained to this great mission of gathering the Lord's sheep into His fold. They will be called and set apart as special witnesses with the express purpose of teaching the fullness of the gospel to those in distant lands.

I was shown that their work will begin toward the end of the tribulations, just prior to and toward the beginning of the building of the New Jerusalem.

In this way, many prophecies of both ancient and modern-day prophets concerning the preaching of the gospel to all the world will come to pass.

Our Day is Comparable to Nauvoo

We need to remember that the Lord's ways aren't necessarily our ways. I enjoy today's modern conveniences, but I realize that changes must take place for Zion to be built.

Our current circumstances are comparable to the Saints living in Nauvoo, Illinois, in the early 1840s. Life was peaceful and comfortable, and missionary work was the emphasis. Many of the Church leaders were serving missions. It seemed the Church would continue to prosper and grow there, and Nauvoo would become a major city.

However, the Prophet Joseph Smith had foretold that the Saints would soon go to the Rocky Mountains. An 1840 letter to the Saints preserves Joseph Smith's prophecy about "a place of safety preparing for them away towards the Rocky Mountains." Throughout the Nauvoo period the Prophet collected information and prepared for a latter-day Zion to be established in the tops of the Rocky Mountains, and several diaries record Joseph Smith's February 1844 instructions to the Quorum of the Twelve Apostles to lead an expedition to the West to locate a new home for the Saints.

Most of the Saints were happy in a prosperous Nauvoo and not anxious to leave after enduring several challenging moves during the previous decade. They were building nice homes and establishing a variety of businesses. Nauvoo was becoming a vital city along the Mississippi River, and although there was occasional trouble with state officials, it felt like things were finally on track for the Church to put down roots.

Much like today, the average member of the Church knew little about the Prophet's plans or the prophecy that had been given concerning the Rocky Mountains. The time hadn't come to emphasize that message. Instead, the Prophet Joseph spent much time giving powerful doctrinal sermons such as the King Follett Discourse that emphasized eternal principles, spiritual growth, and completing the Nauvoo Temple.

We are currently in a similar situation where prophecies have been made about troubled times, but the main emphasis of our Church leaders at this moment is to bring as many souls to the shelter of the gospel as possible before the storm clouds arrive.

We need to remember that we each have an individual plan and that whatever happens is part of the Lord's plan for us. It is imperative that we put our faith and trust in the Lord. Nothing is coincidental.

Some will be called to gather together, while some will be asked to stay behind. Others will stay of their own choosing, and some will not even know there is a gathering. Some will be called on as martyrs—LDS members as well as other believers who are not of our faith. Many will be called to sacrifice and serve. Some will be led to the gospel in this life, while others will be taught the gospel in the next.

All of this is part of the Lord's Great Plan of Happiness, so we just need to do the best we can to do our part and leave the rest to the Lord. I have had dozens of people contact me who have shared personal experiences regarding their promptings and impressions to prepare in some way. Many have wondered why some have had promptings to prepare and others have not. There could be several reasons why this is the case, but it really is not for us to judge. It is up to us to do our part to prepare the best we can for what we need to do. Along the way we need to do our best to help and serve all of the Lord's children in love.

This Era is a Huge Piece of the Puzzle

The emphasis on "hastening the work" is a huge piece of the puzzle as we prepare for future events. We have been blessed with knowledge of certain gospel truths, and we have a responsibility to do all we can to spread the word of God and to testify of these things to our family, friends and neighbors.

Time is short. The Lord is indeed hastening His work. He will continue to do so at an ever increasing rate. As the powers of darkness increase in intensity and power, so will the powers of light. Those on the earth as well as those in heaven will continue to sense and feel the changes that are going on all around them. There will come a point in time when there will be no mistaking which side of the battle we are on and who we have chosen as our Master.

As our faith is tested in every way and on every level, we will be given the choice to learn to trust the Lord in all things. We will be given the choice to follow the Lord in all things, regardless of cost, and to keep the covenants we have made. We may be asked to sacrifice all we have, even our very lives if necessary. In the end, we will be given the choice to choose Christ over all else.

CHAPTER THREE

The Power of Family History and Temple Work

Another aspect of the "hastening of the work" is performing sacred ordinances in the temple for our deceased ancestors. One of the main reasons is because when we do Family History work and complete those ordinances for them, we essentially open the gate for our ancestors who are in Spirit Prison. We are literally freeing our ancestors from bondage and giving them the opportunity to enter Paradise. They gain increased power to help us here on earth with our challenges.

President Thomas S. Monson said, "There are thousands upon thousands, yes, millions upon millions of spirit children of our Heavenly Father who have lived here, who have never heard of the word "Christ," who have died, who have gone back to the Spirit World in their state of progression and have been taught the gospel; and now they are awaiting the day when you and I will do the research which is necessary to clear the way, that we might likewise go into the house of God and perform that work for them, that they, themselves, cannot perform. Are we willing to accept that challenge? My brothers and sisters, I testify that the Lord will bless you as you do accept and respond to that challenge." (*Teachings of Thomas S. Monson*, p. 115-116)

It is not called Spirit Prison because it is like prisons we have on earth. That is just a name given for the realm in the Spirit World where people live who have not yet accepted the gospel. There is a veil of sorts that keeps those in Spirit Prison from crossing over to Paradise. The people in Spirit Prison either have not yet been taught the gospel of Christ, or they have chosen not to accept the gospel. Those who do accept the gospel of Jesus Christ are unable to continue to progress in some areas in the Spirit World until they have received their temple ordinances.

There are areas of varying degrees of light and dark within the Spirit World. Those spirits of the light, just like those here on earth, do not "hang out" with those of the dark. However, there are many from Paradise who spend at least some of their time as missionaries teaching the gospel in Spirit Prison.

As we complete our ancestors' temple work, they are able to enter Paradise and contribute more to the Lord's team. They are able to receive greater light and knowledge, and they are endowed with power to assist us during our mortal lives.

This increase in light and knowledge not only helps them continue to progress in the spirit realm, it also gives them an opportunity to learn more about how to help us here on earth. Those on the other side of the veil continue to progress in many ways. The more light and knowledge we obtain, the greater our awareness and ability to withstand the adversary.

Temples in the Spirit World

I was shown that there are also temples throughout the Spirit World. In those temples, sacred ordinances are performed that are similar to those done on earth. These ordinances allow the spirits there to demonstrate their willingness to accept what is being done in their behalf. However, the ordinances we conduct in our temples here on earth must be done before those ordinances in the Spirit World can be completed. That is one of the reasons the spirits there are so anxious for us to do our part.

Much like missionary work here on earth, the bulk of the temple work will cease for a time when calamities strike across the world. I did see a few "tent temples" in the Places of Refuge, but my understanding is that the majority of the work being done there was likely for people receiving their own ordinances, rather than work for the dead. So the time is now for a great wave of temple work to be completed.

Our Ancestors Are Anxiously Waiting

Our ancestors are aware of the difficult times that are coming. They know this will affect the Saints' ability to do temple work, so they are anxious to reach Paradise before the calamities strike. They don't want to be stuck in Spirit Prison longer than they have to. They realize that once the troubles begin, it might be several years before temple work gets rolling again in the New Jerusalem and the Cities of Light.

I wouldn't be surprised if you have felt promptings to research certain areas of your family history. Just imagine how your great-grandma must feel if she lived a good Christian life but had never heard the message of the restored gospel during mortality. Now she has wholeheartedly accepted it in the Spirit World and is eager to move on to Paradise. Her descendants are now members of the LDS Church, but unfortunately they haven't bothered to see if her temple work has been done, despite spending hours on the computer each day.

According to a *Church News* article published in August 2013, only 25 percent of Church members have at least registered on FamilySearch, and studies show that in a year-long span, only eight percent of Church members have logged on and used FamilySearch. Are you part of the eight percent?

President Monson's Recent Message

President Thomas S. Monson emphasized temple work in the First Presidency message of the June 2014 *Ensign*. He said, "We, as spirit children of our Heavenly Father, were sent to earth at this time that we might participate in hastening this great work.

"The Lord has never, to my knowledge, indicated that His work is confined to mortality. Rather, His work embraces eternity. I believe He is hastening His work in the spirit world. I also believe that the Lord, through His servants there, is preparing many spirits to receive the gospel. Our job is to search out our dead and then go to the temple and perform the sacred ordinances that will bring to those beyond the veil the same opportunities we have."

President Monson added, "We are going to make mistakes, but none of us can become an expert in family history work without first being a novice. Therefore, we must plunge into this work, and we must prepare for some uphill climbing. This is not an easy task, but the Lord has placed it upon you, and He has placed it upon me.

"As you pursue family history work, you are going to find yourself running into roadblocks, and you are going to say to yourself, 'There is nothing else I can do.' When you come to that point, get down on your knees and ask the Lord to open the way, and He will open the way for you. I testify that this is true."

Building the Lord's Army

I know that this work is essential to our salvation. I know that temple and family history work are part of God's eternal plan of happiness for his children. I know that the Lord is hastening his work in all areas in preparation for the Second Coming of our Lord and Savior Jesus Christ.

We need to do all we can to help as many of our brothers and sisters as we can. In so doing, we in turn help ourselves.

Temple work and family history work benefit every single one of God's children. When we engage in this work, we are building the Lord's kingdom here upon the earth as well as in the spirit realm. We are truly building the Lord's army. We are strengthening our forces in preparation for the final battle and are enlisting ourselves and others in the cause of Zion.

CHAPTER FOUR

Don't Delay Getting Your Life in Order

We must not delay getting our lives in order. The time is now to get our houses in order and prepare for the days ahead. Time is short and we must do all in our power to prepare in every needful way. We must do all we can to seek the Lord and learn what He would have us do.

Many of us have been counseled for years to prepare for the days that are upon us. We have been warned again and again of the need to be vigilant in our pursuit of all that is good and is of the light. We have been counseled to prepare both spiritually and temporally for the difficulties that lie at our doorsteps.

Elder Russell M. Nelson spoke to Brigham Young University graduates in August 2014 about the importance of being fully engaged in the work of the Lord. He said that the days are gone of being a quiet and comfortable Christian.

He added, "Your religion is not just about showing up for church on Sunday. It is about showing up as a true disciple from Sunday morning through Saturday night—24/7. There is no such thing as a 'part time' disciple of the Lord Jesus Christ." (*Church News*, August 24, 2014, p. 3)

Many of us have heard these warnings so many times and in

so many ways that we have grown weary of hearing them. Perhaps in some cases we have heard the message so often that we have begun to tune it out. For some it has become mere "background noise," and yet for others it does not even register anymore.

There are others however, who have heard and listened to the messages, and who are being vigilant in their ongoing preparations. These individuals are awakened to the signs all around us, and they are actively preparing for the difficulties we will soon face. They are being obedient to the Lord's commandment to prepare every needful thing.

Those who have yet to have their hearts and minds opened, I want to express with all of my soul the importance of this message. We do not have long until the things that have been prophesied in the scriptures come to pass. We are in the final hours preparatory to the Lord's return. There is much to be done.

A Matter of a Few Years

Within a matter of a few years, it is my belief that the Saints will be called to gather. It will not be long after that before foreign troops will invade America and the earth will erupt in chaos. The heavens will let loose and the powers of darkness will rage.

There will be natural disasters on a mass scale unlike anything the earth has ever experienced before. Earthquakes, hurricanes, tornados, tsunamis, plagues, droughts, famines, pestilence, and all manner of disease will be upon the earth in such a deep and broadened scale that mankind cannot even imagine what it will be like. The seas will become death traps. The world as we know it will cease to exist. Now is the time for us to get our affairs in order, heed the counsel of our prophets and apostles, and follow the warnings of the Spirit. We must prioritize our relationships with the Lord and with our families, and we must seek to do all we can to prepare temporally and spiritually for the days ahead.

The Start of the Breakdown

Heber C. Kimball, First Counselor to President Brigham Young, saw our current situation. He said: "After a while the gentiles will gather by the thousands to this place, and Salt Lake City will be classed among the wicked cities of the world. A spirit of speculation and extravagance will take possession of the Saints, and the results will be financial bondage. Persecution comes next and all true Latter-day Saints will be tested to the limit. Many will apostatize and others will be still, not knowing what to do... Before that day comes, however, the Saints will be put to tests that will try the integrity of the best of them. The pressure will become so great that the more righteous among them will cry unto the Lord day and night until deliverance comes." (*Deseret News*, Church Department, p. 3, May 23, 1931)

As this quote demonstrates, it is my understanding that things will start to fall apart before the Saints gather. We will not be spared all of the troubles and heartaches that will come.

Some events that Elder Kimball foresaw are already happening, while other trials are about to begin. The important thing is to be prepared from this point on so that when the Prophet speaks, you are ready both temporally and spiritually to heed his counsel.

To illustrate, if you look in the scriptures, there are patterns we can find. For example, take the story of Lot and his wife. The Lord warned Lot in advance that he was going to destroy Sodom and Gomorrah. When He told Lot it was time to go, they got out quickly. They were told not to look back. Lot's wife did, and was turned into a pillar of salt. This is a lesson for all of us.

A similar thing happened when Lehi led his family out of Jerusalem. He knew for many years the day would come when they would depart, and they prepared for it. When the Lord finally told them that it was time to leave, they had to act quickly and obediently.

Some may not realize that Jerusalem was not destroyed right away. It was several years after Lehi left Jerusalem when the Lord destroyed the city, but by then Lehi's family was safely in another part of the world.

Let us remember that Noah preached repentance and tried to prepare the people for nearly 120 years. That is no different than for us today. If you look at the history of the LDS Church, we have been given guidance and warnings for many decades now. Will we be ready when the time arrives?

Have Patience in the Camps

We need to have our preparations in order and not hesitate. We need to make sure that when it is time to leave, we do not look back. We know what happens to those who look back. It is not pretty.

This is critical to remember because I was shown that there are going to be people who do this very thing. I was shown the meeting when the prophet invites the Saints to gather. Many will say, "They've got to be kidding! I'm not going to leave. I've got a job, and everything is fine. There is no trouble here."

Then there will be those stalwart individuals who know how to trust their God, who trust their leaders, and who have learned to discern the truth.

I was shown that some will go out of mere obedience, but living in the camps will not be easy. There will come a time when staying in the camps will require great faith, in part because the destructions don't happen the day after we get to camp.

We will feel an urgency as we make our way to the camps, and in some parts of the country it will be for good reasons. I was shown that as we settle in, we are going to get news that nothing really big has happened yet. We will have ways of communicating with the outside world, and we'll be waiting to hear of a major earthquake, or that foreign troops have invaded the coasts. It will seem as if we have been fooled somehow into gathering.

Many will ask themselves, "What am I doing here? I have a perfectly nice home, nice car, and a hot shower." They will say to others, "I could sure use a bath and it's only two hours away. Why am I camping in a tent in the middle of nowhere? This is crazy. This is ridiculous."

Sadly, many will leave the camps, and when they leave, they will not be able to come back. I cannot go into more detail on this, other than to say that I saw many different scenarios, including people deciding to leave after only a day or two. Others make it a week or two. One very clear recollection I have is of several people who make it a few weeks before deciding that they will not stick it out. Their timing could not be worse. Shortly thereafter, things turn to chaos. I do not want to be that person.

Make Improvements Now

Don't delay making improvements in your life. The fact is there are many people who are fully prepared to answer the Lord's call. They are financially secure, magnify their church callings, give service, attend the temple regularly, and have the Spirit with them. When you are around them, you feel uplifted. Get to know them, because they are the ones who will be there to help guide, direct and greet you as you arrive at the gathering places. The Lord has placed such people in every ward and stake who are waiting for the Lord's timetable to move forward.

For them, this book is a review, not a revelation.

The rest of us might have a little work to do, though. Maybe you are financially secure, but the idea of going to church every week or holding a calling just doesn't appeal to you.

There are little things we can work on. If you can't go a day without a Diet Coke before getting a massive headache or having the jitters, it might be time to start weaning yourself. Maybe you go to Disneyland every year, but claim you can't afford a year's supply of food.

It is time for us to get our priorities straight. It is time for us to step up to the plate and do all we can to prepare and protect ourselves and our families.

We need to put our faith and trust in the Lord's plan for us. We need to be obedient to the Lord's commandments and rely on the Holy Spirit as our guide. We need to put our fears aside and focus on the light.

Go to the Lord in Prayer

For those who have concerns regarding how and when the call to gather will come, and what to do in those circumstances when the call does come, I say, "Trust the Lord." Go to Him and tell Him of your fears and concerns. Pour your heart out to Him and express your worries. Confide in Him. Ask Him to give you additional light and knowledge pertaining to this topic and anything else you desire to learn and know.

Wait upon the Lord. He will answer you in the way He knows is best for you and at the time He knows is right for you. If you have concerns about spouses, children, siblings, parents, grandchildren, friends—anyone, regarding anything—take that to the Lord in prayer. He will hear your heartfelt prayers and will give you the peace you seek and the answers you need.

I encourage you to remember the importance of listening to and following the counsel of our living prophets. When the time comes to gather, follow the Spirit and do as the Spirit directs. Remember that there is safety in heeding the warnings of the Holy Ghost.

God has a plan for you and each of His children. Even if we don't agree with or understand what that plan is, it is important that we learn to put our faith and trust in the Living God who knows all. He knows the end from the beginning, and He will not lead us astray.

What About Our Family Photos and Records?

Some of our most important possessions are our family photos, journals, and scrapbooks. What do we do about them? What can we do to preserve them? Will we be able to take them with us when we are called to gather? Many people have asked these questions, including me.

While I cannot speak for anyone else, I can share what the Lord has told me. He has told me to continue writing in my journal. He has told me to continue taking pictures. He has told me to continue doing family history work. He has told me that I need to preserve as much as I can on the computer and then copy it onto something small and portable that I can take with me.

He has told me that many of the records will be preserved here on earth, and that others will be preserved in the Heavens. He has told me to be obedient to the counsel we have been given to preserve our documents. He has told me that we will have access to this information in the New Jerusalem and during the Millennium.

He has reminded me again and again of what I was shown in the Book of Life. He has reminded me that everything on earth is recorded in the Heavens. Even if I must temporarily say good-bye to these things, I am not saying good-bye forever. He has shown me that all things will once again be restored to their proper order.

He has reminded me that no matter what happens, I will one day be able to access that information. He has told me not to worry, and that I should do my best and to leave the rest up to Him. He has told me to trust Him and do as the Spirit directs. He has promised me that in so doing, He will protect me and those things that are most sacred and dear to my heart.

Specific Instructions Will Be Given

Many have asked if there will be specific instructions about what to take and what to leave behind. My understanding is yes, there will be specific instructions given. I have not been told all of what those specific instructions will include. I would suggest that where possible, we do what we can to digitize our records. I would suggest that if you have a question or concern about this topic, ask the Lord what actions you should take, and in what order you should take them.

As mentioned previously, the time is now to get our houses in order. I was shown that as the days go on, food prices and other commodity prices are going to skyrocket. Produce, meat and other grocery items will become so expensive that it will become increasingly difficult to provide for our families. There will come a point in time when we will no longer be in a position to stock up on food and other items.

I was shown that this will be due to a combination of things, such as unemployment, underemployment, high prices, food and water shortages, food and water contaminations, gasoline shortages, bank closings, as well as other factors.

I was shown that the contamination from the Japanese nuclear waste would continue to be spread throughout the ocean. I was shown that this nuclear waste has and will continue to radiate and contaminate sea life. I have been warned not to eat any fish or other food that comes from the ocean.

This is a very personal decision, but I know that for me and my family, for the most part we are no longer buying or eating any ocean fish. This was a decision I made a few years ago after having had so many dreams and impressions given to me that I could not deny the reality of the dire situation we are in when it comes to our health and safety. I have been given very real and personal revelation that I am not to eat it, nor am I to feed it to my family.

I was shown that the governments of the world have and will purposefully misrepresent the circumstances surrounding this topic and other food and water safety issues.

Conspiring Men Seek to Destroy America

I was shown that conspiring men will continue to lie to the people regarding safety issues pertaining to food, water, disease, and other harmful substances. I was shown that these safety concerns are due to both natural and man-made causes. Many of the safety issues we have faced and those we will yet face are due to the evil acts of conspiring men and women who seek to gain control of the hearts and minds of the people.

It was made very clear to me that there are many within our ranks of governments, within and without the United States, who are conspiring to destroy America and many other countries. It was made very clear to me that these conspiring men and women have infiltrated every aspect of our society on every level.

These people seek to destroy the Constitution. I was shown that their ultimate goal is to have control and dominion over all the earth. These secret combinations have been working for decades to overthrow the American people and governments all over the world.

I was shown that these wicked men and women have no respect for human life or for the principle of agency. They have enlisted in Satan's cause. They will stop at nothing to achieve their goal. I was shown that the day will come when the forces of darkness will be unleashed like nothing we have ever seen before in the history of this planet.

Additionally, it was made known to me that there are very wicked people in our government and abroad who are conspiring to kill through the use of biological weapons. This includes food and water contamination, plagues and other diseases. They have already developed many of these weapons and are actually using some of them now, just on a smaller scale.

However, I was also shown that the forces of God will be unleashed like a mighty sword and that the light will permeate the darkness. I was shown that the Armies of God will descend upon the wicked, and in the end, truth and light will prevail.

There Will Be Fear and Panic

I believe these wicked people will attempt many events of varying types to induce more fear and panic into the American people. They will continue to push their evil agendas and will do all they can to lead as many as possible to an eventual dependence on them. Their tactics are the same ones the adversary has used from the beginning—power, persuasion, fear, control, dominance, manipulation—and in many cases, as wolves in sheep's clothing pretending to be one's friend and helper when in fact they seek our destruction.

I was shown they will employ any method necessary to deceive those they seek to control and destroy. As they do now, they will continue to have some success with those who are unaware or blinded by their tactics.

Although there will be many casualties, I know without a doubt that the Lord is allowing these things to happen. In time, He will turn events around and eventually all will be well. We just need to remember to do our best to live the best lives we can, given whatever circumstances we find ourselves in, and to do all we can to have faith in a very loving Father in Heaven and His eternal plan for us.

The Lord is in Charge

As we know, God has planned for these things from the beginning. He has orchestrated this and is fully aware of even those who are on opposing sides, both seen and unseen forces. Quite frankly, the wicked know their days are numbered, so they are stepping it up several notches and will continue to do so until the final hour.

That is why the Lord has saved many of his most valiant, faithful, strong and obedient children to live in this day and age and to stand up and be counted on the Lord's side. Never in the history of the world have the forces of darkness or the forces of righteousness been as great and strong as they are today.

My hope is that I can be counted as one who stands on the right side, along with so many others who were foreordained to stand strong and be counted worthy of the tremendous blessings the Lord offers each of us.

CHAPTER FIVE

Spiritual Preparations
Before the Gathering

I have seen some of the days ahead of us, and what we have to look forward to before the Second Coming. There are glorious events about to unfold, but there will also be severe trials.

There will be a day when we will not be able to access modern medication and doctors. We will need our food and water storage, and life as we know it will no longer exist. That is when we will truly rely on our spiritual preparations—our faith, hope and charity—as much as our temporal preparations.

It is not far off. I don't know exactly when, but I have been shown sequences of events. I do know that since I started having dreams and visions about the events of the Last Days—particularly starting in the fall of 1990, and increasingly so after I had my NDE in 2004—many of the events have already happened and "have been checked off the list."

Our need to prepare both temporally and spiritually has never been greater and it is absolutely critical to our survival that we listen to the Spirit and promptly obey. Following the prophet will soon be the difference between life and death in every sense of the word. I know that there will soon come a day when we will be given the choice to put our faith and trust in our Lord and in our living prophets and apostles. I cannot emphasize enough the importance of spiritual preparedness.

It is my belief that if we are not spiritually prepared, then no matter how temporally prepared we may be, our lack of spiritual preparedness will be what causes us the greatest distress.

We Are Spiritual Beings

We are spiritual beings having a temporal experience. When we are spiritually grounded, we are able to withstand the fiery darts of the adversary. When we are spiritually prepared, we are able to handle the difficulties that life brings. When we rely on and trust in the Lord, we are able to let go of the natural man and accept whatever it is we must face and endure.

When we are doing all in our power to follow the Lord and be obedient to His commandments, then we are given the strength and protection we need to overcome our trials. As the Lord says in D&C 82:10, "I, the Lord, am bound when ye do what I say; but when ye do not do what I say, ye have no promise."

We have been promised great blessings. As designed from the beginning, the Lord has provided a beautiful plan of redemption. Through the power of the Atonement we can be healed, cleansed and purified. Through the power of the Atonement we can fulfill our personal life missions, and we have been promised hope for a greater tomorrow. The time is now for us to prepare for that greater tomorrow!

It is up to us to use our agency to do our part to fill our lamps before the Bridegroom comes. These are gifts that are available to every one of us as God's children, and if it is in our best interest for us to be given those gifts, the Lord grants them. There are no shortcuts to this knowledge. It begins with putting our faith and trust in the Living God. It begins with heartfelt prayer.

How does someone go about preparing for these eventualities

in a spirit of faith and not fear? This information can be overwhelming, especially to those who are trying so hard to live up to their privileges and potential and yet are already plagued with anxiety in our relatively peaceful world.

To those who struggle with these thoughts, feelings and emotions, I say to you that I greatly identify. I have personally struggled with anxiety issues. Knowing what I know and having seen what I have seen, I have to make a constant and concerted effort not to dwell on those things which cause me fear. I work vigilantly to focus on the things of the light. I actively work at learning how to discern when the Lord is speaking to me.

Each day I consecrate my heart, my mind and my efforts to the Lord. Multiple times a day I pray for guidance, strength, faith, trust, clarity, understanding and peace. Moment by moment I do what I can to focus my thoughts, words and deeds on the Lord and on His work; and I work tirelessly at being steadfast, obedient, and diligent in my efforts. I have come to accept that this is just how things are. I have come to accept that this is what the Lord means when He says we must "endure to the end."

I testify to you that the more we focus on spiritual promptings, the more natural it becomes for us. In some ways it gets easier because it becomes a natural part of who we are. Due to the nature of life, however, things do not get easier. In fact, in my own life the opposition and difficulties have not only continued, they have increased. But my ability to meet those challenges has increased as I place my faith and trust in God. If we allow Him to, He really does lift our burdens.

The Lord Gives Added Strength

In my experience, in most cases, the trials and adversities do not necessarily go away, but the Lord gives me the added strength, courage and ability to handle the burdens I carry. As we do all we

_. to become temporally and spiritually self-reliant, the Lord gives us additional opportunities for learning and growth. When He sees that we are able to handle what we have been given, He gives us more.

We are given further light and knowledge line upon line, precept upon precept. The Lord will never give us more than we can handle or than what is for our greater good. This applies to trials as well as insight and knowledge. He seeks to do only that which is for our greatest eternal welfare.

So how do we purify our hearts? How do we have confidence that we are at least on the right path? It is my belief that we will begin to know and understand this is happening because we will feel it in our hearts, in our minds and in our souls. We will begin to see the fruits of our labors. We will reap the results through the law of the harvest.

President Thomas S. Monson said, "Decisions are constantly before us. To make them wisely, courage is needed—the courage to say no, the courage to say yes. Decisions do determine destiny.

"I plead with you to make a determination right here, right now, not to deviate from the path which will lead to our goal: eternal life with our Father in Heaven. Along that straight and true path there are other goals: missionary service, temple marriage, Church activity, scripture study, prayer, temple work. There are countless worthy goals to reach as we travel through life. Needed is our commitment to reach them." (*Ensign*, November 2010, p. 68)

Your Patriarchal Blessing

Many active Church members often neglect to take advantage of a priceless spiritual opportunity that the Lord provides—a patriarchal blessing. If you have received one but haven't read it in a while, the time is now to do so. In these crucial days, there may be passages that apply directly to your spiritual preparation for the future.

If you haven't received a patriarchal blessing, don't delay getting one. A patriarchal blessing allows you to gain a sense of what lies ahead for you, and what the Lord expects of you.

President Ezra Taft Benson said, "I would encourage you to receive a patriarchal blessing. Study it carefully and regard it as personal scripture to you—for that indeed is what it is." (*Ensign*, November 1986, p. 82)

Church members should receive a patriarchal blessing as soon as they are spiritually ready, which is often during their early teenage years. If you feel a desire to receive your patriarchal blessing, don't hesitate. A patriarchal blessing is a special gift from Heavenly Father. Once you receive it, live your life so that those promised blessings will be fulfilled.

Some people feel they must wait until the bishop approaches them, but this isn't so. Let your bishop know you would like a patriarchal blessing. He will interview you and help you arrange an appointment with your stake patriarch. The Lord has a personalized message waiting for you.

President Thomas S. Monson said, "Your patriarchal blessing is yours and yours alone. It may be brief or lengthy, simple or profound. Length and language do not a patriarchal blessing make. It is the Spirit that conveys the true meaning. Your blessing is not to be folded neatly and tucked away. It is not to be framed or published. Rather, it is to be read. It is to be loved. It is to be followed.

"Your patriarchal blessing will see you through the darkest night. It will guide you through life's dangers... Your patriarchal blessing is to you a personal Liahona to chart your course and guide your way." (*Ensign*, November 1986, p. 66)

Following the Prophet

Have you ever asked yourself whether you would heed any invitation or commandment the prophet gives in the future? You might be able to see where you stand by working through the following scenario.

We have about 15 million members of the Church. Consider that about half are considered active by attending Sacrament Meeting once a month. But what percentage of those people attend each week? Of that group, how many faithfully fulfill their callings? Then, how many pay a full tithing? How many hold current temple recommends at all times?

Of those who hold recommends, how many attend the temple regularly? (I realize the definition of "regularly" means different things for different people depending on their personal circumstances.)

Now of those individuals, how many have heeded the prophet's counsel of self-reliance and have any food storage and water storage at all? How many have even just a basic 72-hour kit for themselves? How many have at least a three-month supply of food and other goods? How many have more than three months? How many have a full year's supply?

Those who can answer "yes" to most or all of those questions are on the right track. They are a blessing and an example to their wards and families. Most importantly, they are actively working on being temporally and spiritually prepared. They are following the Lord's counsel and will likely continue to heed His words in the future.

A Ripple Effect

The Lord has a plan for each and every one of us. When it comes to spiritual preparations, our thoughts and intentions do matter. They not only impact us personally on every level, but they also influence others. In fact, we are all so interconnected that our thoughts, intentions, and actions have an impact or "ripple effect" on the entire universe. Even if they are on a subconscious level, they are still a form of energy. It is powerful.

We do our part and the Lord does His. His promises are sure. He is no respecter of persons, but He does hold us accountable and requires faithfulness, trust and obedience so that He can fulfill His end of the promise.

CHAPTER SIX

Temporal Preparations Before the Gathering

When it comes to temporal preparations, there are several aspects. I will discuss just a few. The first scenario to consider is a situation where you will have to stay in your home, either due to a quarantine, natural disaster, or even martial law. You would focus on food, water and possible sanitation issues. It is very likely that you would also encounter the need for other basic survival gear and skills in the event that electricity and other modern conveniences are no longer an option.

The other scenario is when the Saints are called to gather at the mountain camps. That is when we will need tents, tools, and other types of supplies.

Where you live should be taken into account. If you live on the tenth floor of an apartment building in a big city, you'll prepare differently than if you live in a small rural town.

Also, some families have felt prompted that their home and property will be an initial gathering place, so they would likely feel the need to have plenty of food and other items on hand for the people who will be coming to stay with them.

I was shown various scenes pertaining to life in the camps and elsewhere. I witnessed my family and others living in these tent cities. I was shown that we left in the early spring of the year, and camped for quite a long time. I saw that we were camping year-round and that the circumstances required us to utilize both cool weather and warm weather clothing.

Live for Today, Prepare for Tomorrow

After being shown many of these things, the message was given to me that I still needed to continue "planting my cherry trees" in my daily life. This means that although it is important for us to do all we can to temporally and spiritually prepare for the days ahead, we still need to live our lives in the present. We can't lose sight of today, and in doing so, we will be better prepared for the future, with whatever experiences that may bring.

It is a balancing act, with moderation in all things. We need to fulfill our obligations at work, home, school, and church, but keep an eye on world events and be ready when trouble arises.

John Taylor had this to say about things to come: "Are we capable, as Latter-day Saints, of fulfilling our destiny on the earth, and procuring a full temporal salvation and sustaining ourselves, on temporal principles without the interposition of the Almighty? I tell you no, we are not, no more than we are in regard to any other things.

"We read in the Scriptures of a time that is coming when there will be a howling among the merchants in Babylon, for men will not be found to buy their merchandise. This is in accordance with the prediction of John the Revelator. And the gold and the silver and the fine linen, etc., in Babylon will be of no avail.

"But before that time comes, we as a people must prepare for those events that we may be able to live and sustain ourselves when in the midst of convulsions that by and by will overtake the nations of the earth, and among others, this nation. The time that is spoken of is not very far distant.

"He that will not take up his sword against his neighbor must needs flee to Zion for safety. And Zion herself must flee to the God of Israel and hide herself in the shadow of his wing, seeking for his guidance and direction to lead her in the right path, both as regards spiritual and temporal affairs; things social and things political, and everything pertaining to human existence.

"We are not prepared as a people today for the accomplishment of this object; we need the interposition and guidance of the Almighty. It is just as necessary that we be under his guidance in relation to these matters." (John Taylor, *Journal of Discourses*, Vol. 21:32-33. April 9, 1879)

Physical Fitness

I have had a few people ask me what I am doing to prepare for the days ahead in terms of personal fitness. I have regularly been working out, but the past year and a half I have put on quite a bit of weight. (This is due to poor eating habits, side effects of medication, and health issues I still struggle with.) I am working at getting the extra weight off.

In particular, I have started walking regularly (since I can't run due to my health). I have also been going hiking. This is particularly important because I know that I will need to walk and hike several miles to a Place of Refuge in the future.

I am still trying to be better about getting to bed earlier. This is an effort for me because I am a natural night owl and like to stay up a bit to have time to myself after the kids go to bed. So I am working on this one! Earlier to bed, and ideally earlier to rise.

Scriptures and Songbooks

After my NDE and several dreams regarding last-day events, I felt impressed to purchase mini combination scriptures for each of our bags, as well as a mini hymnbook and mini Primary songbook for each bag. They add a bit of weight to the bags, but they will be well worth it when the time comes that we need to grab and go.

The scriptures will be essential and the Primary songbooks and hymnbooks will be an added blessing. Think of the early LDS pioneers and how little they could bring with them, but they brought their scriptures to read, and they regularly sang and danced around the campfire. These simple activities brought them joy, unity, increased faith and hope, and lightened their burdens.

Survival Skills

Some have questioned if wilderness survival skills have any value. My answer to this is yes—absolutely. The more we know in this area the better. The same can be said of any knowledge or skill we acquire. We need to be as knowledgeable and skilled in as many areas as possible.

Of course it is unreasonable to think that each of us can become an expert in every area, but we need to do all within our power to learn as much as we can. This is another area that requires our faith and obedience to the Spirit.

I encourage each of us to learn what it is we need to know and develop. I am confident that as we seek to do the Lord's will in all things, and we seek guidance and direction from the Lord, He will help us know what we need to learn and do. It is through the promptings of the Holy Ghost that we know the truth of all things, and this includes knowing what talents, gifts and skills will be of help to us individually and collectively.

Some people are skilled in communications. Others are skilled in sanitation. Some have leadership skills, and others are great at following directions. Many people have been blessed with gifts of the Spirit that will be of great worth. There is an endless list of talents and gifts the Lord has given us and we will use many of them in a variety of settings.

Several individuals have contacted me expressing their concerns about the logistics of their preparations. They are confused as to what they should get, when they should get it, and how it will possibly be utilized. Many have wondered how their food and other supplies will be transported to the camps. They have questioned how much they should buy, what they should buy, how they should store it, and what will become of it all.

Some have wondered, "Will all of my food storage be able to go? Should I still bottle fruit? What about my other supplies? How will we transport everything?"

To these individuals I will say this: I cannot answer those questions for you personally. I do not know what each individual or family circumstance is or will be, and it is not my place to presume that I could even begin to give advice on this.

However, I can share with you what I currently know I need to do for my family, based on what I was shown. I share this with you in hopes that it will give you a basic idea of things I think we will need going forward. Every situation is unique however, so please understand that I am not saying this is what you should get or do. I am simply sharing my thoughts, impressions, and ideas about some of the things the Lord has told my husband and I that we need to obtain for our future survival.

Again, this is not an inclusive list of items. It is simply a suggestion of where one might begin in their preps. For specific guidance and direction, you need to do your own personal study and research. Through prayer we can come to know and learn for ourselves what it is the Lord would have us do, how He would like us to prepare, and in what order and manner we should do these things.

The following list is an example of some of the things my husband and I have felt prompted to get. These items are in no particular order of relevance or importance.

* 72-hour kits packed in backpacks that we can hike with for several hours if need be.

* Minimum of three months of food storage of rotatable goods and other items

* At least one year of food storage per person (preferably more)

* Sanitation supplies, personal hygiene items and kits

* Food preparation items (Dutch Oven, Caste iron pans and skillets, and cooking utensils and items such as oven mitts, can opener, knives, cutting board, etc.)

* Hats for all seasons

* Gloves—several pairs of work gloves and winter gloves

* Sunscreen and bug spray

* Tools—Axes, hammers, nails, screw drivers, screws, hunting knives and others helpful tools useful when camping in a long-term setting

* An all-weather tent which can withstand high winds and storms and that has a vent for a tent stove

* A tent stove for heating and cooking inside the tent during cold winter weather or when otherwise confined to our tent

* Water

* Water purification supplies

* Water storage supplies

* Several tarps

* Lots of rope of various lengths for various purposes

* Clothing for all seasons including winter snow

* Hiking boots

* Snow boots

* Wool socks

* Regular socks

* Tennis shoes and several pairs of "camp shoes"

* Sleepwear

* Underclothing
* Warm bedding (we have winter sleeping bags as well as light weight bags for summer weather)
* Memory foam
* Medication, supplements, essential oils and other supplies that would be helpful in any medical situation (including several first aid kits, suture kit, snake bite kit, etc.)
* Scissors, multi-tools, tweezers, razors, super-glue
* Pots and pans, cups, plates, dishes, silverware
* Wash basins for dishes, cleaning and bathing
* Storage organizers
* A variety of batteries
* Emergency radios and communications equipment
* Personal records, pictures, official documents, such as marriage license, birth certificates, etc.—paper copies as well as scanned versions put on a thumb drive for portability
* Family history records
* Cash—including small bills and coins
* Hymnbooks, Primary song books, other music
* Scriptures
* Camp tables
* Lanterns, matches, a variety of flashlights, candles, and other sources of light and heat
* Written or printed contacts list of family and friends
* Paper maps of various states and regions of the United States
* Laundry detergent, dish soap and hand soap
* Spare tires for the trailer and car
* Various garage tools and household tools and supplies
* Calculators
* Writing utensils
* Pet food and supplies
* Fuel

* Wheat grinder
* Eye wear—several pairs of glasses, contacts, and sunglasses for each family member

Employment Concerns

Some have asked me about whether or not there will be time for individuals to give notice of leaving jobs or businesses. They have expressed concern about leaving situations that could potentially lead to negative results or consequences for others.

My answer to these concerns is simple but sincere. I do not know exactly how and when things will play out. I do not have the specific answers to give to anyone, and the Lord is not going to tell me what to tell others regarding this topic. I do not have stewardship over anyone other than me and my family.

The Lord continues to remind me regarding what I have stewardship over, and that I need to "fine tune" my abilities to discern the Spirit so that I am ready and able and willing to go when called. He tells me that when the time is right, I will know what actions to take and how to handle the responsibilities I have been given.

He has told me that no matter the circumstances I face when the call to gather comes, I need to obey quickly. He has promised me that as I heed the counsel of our living prophets and apostles, I will be guided and protected.

I have had people specifically ask me about certain preparation items, such as what type of tent I recommend. Again, my answer to this question is that you need to research and study these things out on your own and then take your questions and concerns to the Lord. For our situation, we purchased a good-sized canvas tent with a stove vent. This is what the Lord directed us to do. He may very likely direct you to do something different.

We were prompted to purchase a tent that was lighter weight

and more portable than other types of canvas tents. Portability was a priority for us, as was the need for a durable, all-weather tent. Staying within our budget and not going into debt for preparations is also important to us, so we purchase items as we can afford them, without going into debt. Each individual circumstance is different.

Food Comes First

I will say this: I highly recommend that you follow the counsel of our church leaders and get at least your year's supply of food and other items before you purchase a tent or other survival gear. Food comes first. After you are able to get at least a year's supply of food, then I suggest you start working on getting your other supplies.

I am confident in saying that as you follow the counsel of our prophets and apostles, and as you live providently, the way will be made available for you to prepare as you need to. Through your spiritual preparations you will be guided and directed as to what temporal preparations you need to make and the order in which you need to make them.

Avoiding Debt

Many people have asked me about debt. They wonder why it is important to get out of debt if the world economies are ultimately going to fail. Some have been concerned about the debt they carry and have worried that due to their debt they will be unable to gather when the invitation comes.

Many have questioned if it is better for them to pay off their debt as fast as they can, or if they should use what money they do have to purchase food storage and other emergency prep items.

I appreciate these questions, and I can relate personally to the concerns regarding this topic. There are several reasons why we have been continually counseled to get and stay out of debt. The first one that comes to mind is the fact that debt is a very literal bondage. When we have debt, we are limited in our actions. We are burdened by the weight of owing money to someone that we otherwise would be able to save or spend on something else.

There are, of course, different kinds of debt. Consumer debt is different than debt from a home mortgage or student loan. All debt restricts our future action, but consumer debt does affect us differently. I cannot go into great detail here on all of the ways the various kinds of debt keeps us in bondage, but I will share with you my personal feelings and impressions on the matter.

Our prophets and apostles have been called and ordained to serve as Special Witnesses. They are Prophets, Seers, and Revelators. They have been shown many of the things which lie in our future. They have counseled us for years to live providently, to get out and stay out of debt, and to do all in our power to save up stores for the days of tribulation.

We need to listen to them and heed their counsel. We need to get serious about our finances. We need to do all in our power to pay our debts, even if it means we must sacrifice many of the modern conveniences we might otherwise enjoy.

We need to be diligent in obeying the Lord's commandments so that we will be found worthy before the Lord to be able to call upon Him to sustain and protect us in time of need. We need to do our part to pay our debts so that when the time comes for us to heed the call of our living Prophet, there will not be anything to impede our progress.

I am confident in knowing that as we do all within our power to get our houses in order and prioritize the right things, then the Lord will take care of the rest for us. I am confident in testifying that as we follow the counsel of our living Prophet, we will be blessed beyond measure. We will experience tender mercies, a multitude of blessings, and miracles that cannot be denied.

As we honor our covenants, including attending to our debts, we will be filled with a greater capacity to feel of and impart of the Spirit. We will be given greater light and knowledge. Our faith and trust in God's plan will increase. Our eyes will be opened, our ears will hear, and our hearts will be softened. We will feel an increase in His love, and in turn we will increase in our love for others. As the chains of debt are loosed, we will feel an increase of the Lord's influence in our lives.

Our ability to focus on that which matters most will increase and intensify and we will find that our hearts and minds are turned more toward God and His eternal purposes, rather than the material possessions we own, or the temporal things we are often distracted with and by. As we put our faith and trust in God and in His servants, we can be uplifted and edified. We can experience the joy that comes from the freedom of living a provident life.

My husband and I are doing what we can to prepare in all ways, but we aren't going into further debt to do so. It's a difficult balancing act because resources are limited. However, when we feel prompted to do something, then we need to act without hesitation.

I do know that I have been shown that the government will come in and take things—homes, cars, and other property. We feel it best to first have all credit card debt paid off, and cars, then the other things like student loans and homes. I encourage each of us to follow the counsel of the prophets and continue to listen to the Spirit on this. It is very important to avoid debt wherever and whenever possible.

Places of Refuge

I have had several people ask whether I saw Places of Refuge or Cities of Light in certain areas of the country, and even in other parts of the world. My answer to this is yes. I have seen hundreds of tent cities all over the world, many dozens of Places of Refuge, and perhaps a half dozen of the Places of Refuge that later become Cities of Light. I am not suggesting that I have seen all of them. I was shown specific places, for specific purposes. I was given a general understanding as to why I was shown these places, but that knowledge has been given to me for reasons specific to my purpose and mission in life, and it is not something I have permission to go into with more detail.

I did see tent cities and Places of Refuge throughout the world, with the majority of those I was shown being in the United States. It was made known to me however, that the Lord has and is preparing similar places all over the world, not just within the United States.

I was shown that the Saints in Central and South America flee to the mountains of their countries for refuge. I was shown the Saints gathering throughout Europe and Canada. I saw people gathering for safety in various parts of Africa, Asia, and the Middle East. I witnessed gatherings in New Zealand, Australia, China, Russia, and elsewhere.

Some of the gatherings were organized by the LDS Church, and others were organized by different faiths. Many people gathered together in large tent cities of their own accord. I was shown there were many reasons people chose to gather, including for safety and protection from war, plague, pestilence, drought, famine, and natural disaster.

Transportation to the Gathering Places

Many people have asked for more clarification on the topic of transportation to the gathering places. Previously I have shared that I saw that some people were taken by bus, and others drove their own vehicles to the camps. I do not have a great deal of knowledge about this specific topic. I do have a basic understanding that where you live will play a role in how you travel to the camps, but I don't know how the transportation decisions are made and who will or won't take buses versus other vehicles.

I do know that the LDS Church will send large white semi-trucks to various designated locations for loading and distribution of food storage and some other items.

I have been shown that some of us will be called to gather for a while in one location, and then later we will be called to move to another location to join with other groups. This will not happen immediately. This relocation process will occur after several months of living in the first camp.

Some have expressed concern about the ability to connect with family members who are serving in the missionary field, or who do not heed the initial call to gather to places of safety. They have asked what I know about the process of locating and reconnecting with these loved ones.

Unfortunately, this is a topic I do not have complete clarity on. Every time I have prayed for answers pertaining to this topic, the Lord has simply directed me to trust in Him and in His plan, and to encourage others to do likewise.

Several people have expressed concern about food allergies and sensitivities, as well as other health issues that create difficulties and limitations. I have been asked if I feel they should store organic, non-GMO, gluten-free food. My response to this is the same I have given for many other inquiries—ask the Lord.

Healing Miracles

I do know that in time, many in the camps will experience great healing miracles. I have been shown that many people will be healed not only from allergies and food intolerances, but also from life-threatening illnesses and disease. I have also been shown that not all are healed, and that our faith is severely tested in every possible way.

I have been asked if we will be able to eat our own food in the tent cities or Places of Refuge. The answer to this is yes and no, depending on where you go. In some of the tent cities people will be left to survive off of their own supplies, but in the Places of Refuge, we will live off of our own supplies as well as the collective whole.

In the Places of Refuge, in order to survive for the duration, at some point in time we will have to pool our resources together and learn to work and live in harmony with one another.

I saw that this was a great trial and test of faith for many, and that there were quite a few misunderstandings and disputations among the people. I saw that some people chose to leave the camps because they were unable to reconcile their differences.

I saw that some people left the camps because they refused to unify. I saw that some people left the camps because they felt they could better survive on their own with their own provisions, rather than share their limited resources with others. I also saw that in time, the hearts of many of the people were softened and changed. In a miraculous way, as faith and trust in the Lord increased, so did our provisions.

For those who stayed and endured the many hardships, through their faith, the Lord provided miracle after miracle. Food was replenished when it seemed all was lost. Health was restored when it seemed death was imminent. Safety and security abounded when it seemed no escape was possible.

I saw that there will be many people who will pass away during this time, but those who have been foreordained to prepare the way of the Savior's Second Coming will be able to fulfill their missions—whether on this side of the veil or on the other side. The Lord is over all, and He will use the talents and gifts He has given us to build his Kingdom on the earth and into the eternities.

Of greatest importance is the need for us to remember that the Lord has a great plan for every one of His beloved children, and it is up to us to trust in Him and follow Him, no matter the trials and tribulations we are called upon to endure.

CHAPTER SEVEN

Church Leaders Will Prepare the Saints

We truly live in perilous times, but I am grateful for the knowledge that the Lord has provided a way for the Saints to be warned of approaching danger.

I appreciate the following statement by President Gordon B. Hinckley: "The Church is true. Those who lead it have only one desire, and that is to do the will of the Lord. They seek His direction in all things. There is not a decision of significance affecting the Church and its people that is made without prayerful consideration, going to the fount of all wisdom for direction. Follow the leadership of the Church. God will not let his work be led astray." (*Ensign*, November 1983, p. 46)

Our leaders will prepare us for upcoming changes in our daily lives. As troubles come, it is quite possible that Church properties across the world will become "holy places" to the Saints in those particular areas as times get tougher. Wherever there is a stake of Zion, there will be a place of refuge established, whether it is in Africa, Europe, South America or elsewhere. Their establishment will always come through the prophet and proper priesthood channels.

If you are active in the Church, you will not be caught

unaware. Ahead of any actual gatherings, Church leaders will take inventory of their wards and stakes and evaluate which families can be expected to participate.

My understanding is that there will be inquiries from our local leaders about our preps before the actual call to places of refuge. As time draws closer, these inquiries and other things will help us to know the time to gather is imminent. I have been told that in my case, the Spirit will prompt and warn me in advance. This is dependent, of course, on my obedience and diligence in doing all I can to live worthy of receiving the Spirit in my life.

Knowledge is Being Poured Out

I have been contacted by several people who have seen many of the same things that I was shown concerning the future. Some were shown these things during their own NDEs, while others have been shown in dreams and visions. Many people have been given some of this knowledge through other forms of personal revelation, such as thoughts and impressions that have come into their minds. Several have shared knowledge imparted to them through their patriarchal blessings. People from all walks of life have felt prompted to prepare both spiritually and temporally. The Lord is warning us in many ways.

President Joseph Fielding Smith said, "Knowledge will be poured down upon this people, and the Lord will make known unto us from time to time, through revelation, and the Spirit of inspiration, many things that are for our good, when we are prepared and ready to receive them. I speak generally of the Church." (*Doctrines of Salvation*, Vol. 1 , p. 244)

I know without a doubt that the Lord loves us. He knows us individually by name. He cares about us and what happens to us. He wants us to be happy, find joy, and learn what we came here to learn. He wants us to return to our heavenly home and receive all of the blessings we have been promised.

It is up to us to choose what part we will play in building His kingdom. We must decide whether or not we will join Him in carrying out His great plan. Whether we choose to help Him build His Kingdom or not, He will succeed. In the end, no matter the opposition, God and His people will be victorious.

Though the battles may be fierce and the casualties great, the Lord will win this battle. He knows all. He sees all. He hears all. There is nothing too great or too small for the Lord. Through our faith and obedience to the Lord's commandments, we will be protected.

This does not mean that we will not face hardship and difficulty, or not be called upon to endure great adversity and persecution. In reality, few will be spared from war, pestilence, disease, or any other calamity.

It does mean that through our faith we will be protected spiritually, and in some cases it does mean we will literally be protected physically. However, it is a misconception to think that if we are faithful and obedient we will be spared from the imminent trials of the last days.

In fact, we have been promised the opposite. We have been told that the Lord's people must endure great trials and adversities in preparation for the Lord's return. We have been warned that we will be called upon to suffer and endure the "refiner's fire" in order to become a Zion people.

It is true that the Lord is preparing Places of Refuge for the Saints. We will be invited to gather together to seek refuge from the storm. It is also true that in gathering we will find great protection and we will experience and witness incredible miracles, but we will still be called upon to endure much.

The Lord's prophets and apostles have been warning us of these upcoming events for many years. We have been given counsel repeatedly about the need to prepare temporally and spiritually. We have been told to get our houses in order. We have been encouraged to do all within our power to seek the Lord and His spirit. Some of us have been obedient in heeding this counsel. Others of us have been slow to hear the words of the Prophets and we have delayed our preparations. Still others have yet to learn of these things.

Difficult Questions

Many have asked questions such as the following: "When we are called to gather, what do people do about their jobs? What about school? What if we own a business? Does the church close their school campuses? How does the 'world' respond to our up and leaving? What does the media say?"

I wish I could answer those questions specifically and others like them. I cannot. I have a basic idea of how I think some things will play out, but those are just my own opinions based on what I have been shown and what I have felt.

I will not go into more detail concerning these things. I do not have stewardship beyond my own family, and I do not have permission from the Lord to discuss things in such detail. It would be wrong of me to even try to attempt to do so.

As I have mentioned many times before, we need to be prayerful and take our questions and concerns to the Lord. If and when He decides it is in our best interest to know things, He will tell us. Otherwise, we need to have faith and trust in Him and in His eternal plan for us, whatever that may be.

Shelters Prepared by the Church

I was shown the Church started preparing temple grounds and shelters as the first worldwide problems began to occur. I saw that these shelters were scattered across the nation and even the world.

This is in keeping with Doctrine and Covenants Section 45, which reads, "And there shall be men standing in that generation, that shall not pass until they shall see an overflowing scourge; for a desolating sickness shall cover the land. But my disciples shall stand in holy places, and shall not be moved; but among the wicked, men shall lift up their voices and curse God and die." (D&C 45:31-32)

In Doctrine and Covenants 101:21-22 we learn that these "holy places" are the stakes of Zion, and certainly also include the Church's actual temples and church buildings.

The Trials of Our Day

Brigham Young foresaw our day and the unique challenges we face. At this moment in time, our prosperity is the biggest obstacle for some of us. We truly enjoy our comfortable homes, peaceful neighborhoods, leisure activities, and technological toys. Those things are fine, as long as we stay true to our covenants, serve faithfully in the Church, and commit in our hearts that we will follow the Prophet no matter what, even if it means giving up these luxuries.

President Young said, "It is our duty to preach the gospel, gather Israel, pay our tithing, and build temples. The worst fear that I have about this people is that they will get rich in this country, forget God and his people, wax fat, and kick themselves out of the Church and go to hell. This people will stand mobbing, robbing, poverty and all manner of persecution, and be true. My greater fear for them is that they cannot stand wealth; and yet they have to be tried with riches, for they will become the richest people on this earth." (Nibley, *Brigham Young*, p. 128)

President Gordon B. Hinckley commented on this quote by saying, "I believe that day, spoken of by Brigham Young with a voice of prophecy that rose above the voices of defeat and criticism, has come. We have been blessed with the bounties of heaven and the bounties of earth. Oh, how magnificently we have been blessed! Now, with gratitude in our hearts, let us not dwell upon the few problems we have. Let us rather count our blessings and in a great spirit of gratitude, motivated by a great faith, go forth to build the kingdom of God in the earth." (*BYU Speeches*, October 29, 1974)

I find comfort in knowing that our Church leaders are filled with faith and confidence in our turmoil-filled world. They are guiding us even now, and will continue to give us the guidance we need at the proper time.

President Joseph Fielding Smith said, "The Lord has not left us helpless. There has never been a time since the restoration of the gospel when we have not had a prophet, someone to lead us, to direct us, to teach us the commandments of God that we might walk in the strait and narrow path. We are not without leaders; and the time shall never come when the Lord will not find someone that he can trust, in whom he has confidence, and who will be qualified to stand to represent him among the people." (*Doctrines of Salvation*, Vol. 1, page 242)

At this point in time, building a strong testimony, following the commandments, and actively participating in the Church's programs are the ways to spiritually "stand in holy places."

At some point, though, those prophecies will become more literal, and our Church leaders will guide and direct the church members to safety. I am grateful for that knowledge.

CHAPTER EIGHT

The Prophet's Invitation to Gather

My understanding is that the call to gather will come before things in society get really dangerous or threatening. There will be some natural disasters, economic turmoil, and continuing moral decay in the near future, but the slide down the slippery slope to chaos will begin gradually.

In fact, as a society we are already starting down the slope, but we keep telling each other, "Hey, things will start looking up again soon," even as we see nothing but a downhill path into darkness ahead of us.

In other words, when the prophet invites us to gather, things will not be much different than they are today. The foreign troops arriving and the major destructions will not have happened yet, which is one of the reasons it will take so much faith and obedience for people to leave behind their homes, jobs, friends, and comforts of life.

The "gathering" is not a rescue mission after the major calamities have started. It is a call to action for the Saints to gather in faith and obedience to the Prophet's counsel. The call to gather will be issued as an invitation, not as a commandment from the Lord.

I was shown that the invitation to gather will be issued by the First Presidency of the Church. As I mentioned in the previous chapter, we will be given additional instruction and counsel from our Church leaders prior to the actual invitation to gather. The invitation will not be done in haste. It has been well-planned and thought-out. The Lord has been preparing our Church leaders and many others for several years.

A Letter and a Broadcast

It is my understanding that when the right time comes, the First Presidency of the Church will send a letter to each of the Stakes, similar to what has been done when other official church business has been conducted. The letter from the First Presidency will be given to the Bishops of each ward, with instructions on when and how the letter is to be read over the pulpit during Sacrament meeting.

In part, I saw that this letter will include an invitation for members to attend a special meeting at designated church buildings. The letter also includes the date and time of the meeting and basic instructions pertaining to some of what will be discussed at the meeting. It is my understanding that emphasis will be given to Church members on the importance of attending the meeting and of being on time.

I was shown that in my area, the meeting will include a special broadcast from the First Presidency of the Church. The invitation to gather will come directly from the First Presidency and there will be an opportunity for members to communicate with others about some of what was discussed in the meeting.

Prior to the meeting, we will be allowed to invite all who are interested to attend the meeting later that night. That is the crucial time. I was shown that there were ushers standing in the doorways of the church buildings, welcoming people to the meeting, similar to when we have a temple dedication.

I saw that the doors remained unlocked for five or ten minutes after the hour, but as soon as the broadcast began, the doors of the church building were locked and no one else was allowed inside for the duration of the meeting.

People were permitted to leave the building. However, if they chose to leave, they were not allowed back in until after the meeting was over.

During the meeting, the prophet shared confidential information concerning the Church's preparations, and then he issued the invitation for the Saints to gather. Once the invitation was given, we were asked to go home and immediately begin packing up our food storage and other specified items to be transported to Places of Refuge.

The turn-around time we were given was quick—less than twenty-four to forty-eight hours in most cases. I do not know if that will be the scenario for every stake, but once the invitation is given, there will not be much time to spare.

I was shown that the majority of Church members will not heed the call to gather. This is due a number of reasons, but the impression I had is because they are not prepared to hear the message. Many simply do not have the faith to go. Some simply refuse to believe it, and many even think it is a crazy idea. Others allow their fears and insecurities to cloud their judgment. There are those who even come to the church buildings to mock and laugh at those who chose to heed the call. Skeptics convince others to ignore the invitation. Thankfully, the faithful Saints will ignore the naysayers and complete their preparations.

Specific Gathering Locations

As I mentioned, the Church's implementation of the gathering will be very organized. People will be assigned to go to specific camp locations that were previously built and prepared for this event. My understanding is that for the most part the camps will be organized by Stakes, but I do not know the details of how that is to be done. I have not been shown where certain Stakes are assigned, or which Stakes will be grouped together.

It was made clear to me that the call for our family to gather happened in the early Spring of the year. One scene I specifically remember is seeing us loading food storage boxes into a large white semi-truck provided by the LDS Church. We were at a church building in the wee hours of the morning, attempting to load the items before sunrise.

In this scene and others, the air was a bit chilly. There were patches of snow on the ground, but not much. It looked as if we were on the tail end of a large snowfall and most of the remaining snow had already melted. As we loaded the trucks, we could see our breath in the air.

In another scene I saw people at a building loading various supplies. Again, I saw the Church's huge white semi-trucks there. This scene was during the day, but still in the morning hours. There was a real sense of urgency about their work. It was not made known to me the location of this scene, but I was left with the distinct impression that similar scenes were being played out in several other areas across the country.

My Family Initially Stays Behind

I was shown that in my family's case, we will be living in the Midwest, and we were asked to stay behind to help others as they came through the Kansas City area on their way to their assigned locations. During this time, things in the country started to deteriorate, and we were feeling antsy to go to a camp.

When it was finally our time to depart, we were given very specific instructions as to the driving route we were to take, places to avoid, and other information that was critical to our journey to ensure our safe arrival at our designated camp.

I was shown that we traveled in a caravan to Utah with some of our extended family and others from our stake in Kansas. As I explained in *A Greater Tomorrow*, we were assigned a particular camp in the Rocky Mountains. The logical route would have been to take I-70, but we journeyed from the Kansas City area in a southern direction to avoid Denver, which had become too dangerous for travelers. So we drove through Texas, New Mexico, Arizona, and then into Utah. I saw us pass through the Moab area, then proceed north through Price Canyon in central Utah. When we entered Price Canyon, there were men there to help us through safely.

I saw that when we arrived in Utah County, we went our separate ways and each stayed at different locations for a night or two. My husband and I and our three children stayed with some of my extended family for a night while we recovered a bit from our long drive to Utah.

The following day, we said good-bye to my family members and we left in our own vehicle to drive north up I-15. We traveled for at least a few hours, because I saw us drive up Sardine Canyon to the city of Logan, and then beyond. I was not shown the rest of our journey or where we ended up. In the next scene, we had arrived at our destination and were parking our car. Men on horseback were there to meet us and to help us. They informed us that we had a long hike ahead of us.

I was given the understanding that many of our supplies we had brought with us were going to be taken to the camps by these men on horseback. Some things we were going to come back for later.

We were given a map and basic directions on how to hike in to the camp. We were counseled to hike at a steady pace so that we could arrive at the camp before nightfall. We used the map and directions given to us, as well as compasses, to figure out where we were going. We hiked most of the day, stopping for a brief time to eat a quick lunch, and then continued on our way in order to make it to the camp before sunset.

We arrived at camp just in time to get settled in and have dinner before it got late. We were met by several people who had been expecting our arrival, but I did not recognize any of them. So I do not know exactly who we were camping with or why we had been grouped with those people.

It was made clear to me that the camp was already set up and well-organized. I could see there were a few large tents. At least one was being used for storage items, including food. Others were being used for gathering groups together for various purposes.

Will We Be With Our Family Members?

Several people have contacted me regarding concerns about various family members and their desires to reside in the same camps. They have asked me what I know about this and what my understanding is on how the camps are organized in this regard. Again, I wish I could answer that question, but I cannot. I have not been given that information, but it is my personal opinion that since the Lord's church is organized by stakes, we will likely be organized by stakes when we camp.

I also know that the family is the central unit in God's plan of happiness and redemption. I know that the Lord loves us and we have been taught that the family is of utmost importance. So it also makes sense to me that there will be some who will be assigned to camps with their families. Again, this is just my personal opinion, so please take it only as that. I really do not know who will be assigned where or how that is to be done.

I know this topic is of great concern to many people. Some have worried that they would not be able to camp with their family members, and others have worried that they *will* have to camp with their family. I too have pondered this very topic, and have petitioned the Lord to know more about how things will play out for my family during that time.

The answer the Lord continues to give me is that I must trust in Him and know that whatever happens, no matter where we end up, it will be the right place, at the right time, for the right reasons. He continues to tell me to have faith in Him and in His plan for me, knowing that everything that happens to me and my family is for our greater good.

The Elderly and Infirm

Many have been concerned about the elderly and the infirm. They have worried about what will happen to these people and to others who have specific health issues requiring medical treatment that may or may not be available in the camps.

I have also had concerns about this. What I have been shown is that great miracles will occur. I have been shown that some do pass on from mortality, but many are healed from life-threatening diseases and illnesses. I was shown that through the power of the priesthood and the faith of the people, many are healed, protected, purified, cleansed, and sanctified.

I was shown that when supplies of modern medicine run out, more people will open their hearts to alternative health care methods. I saw that when alternative health care methods didn't seem to work or were no longer available, then more people opened their hearts to the healing power of the priesthood, resulting in true miracles.

I was shown that in many cases, people will eventually learn to have deeper faith and trust in God. They will call upon God and His angels to protect, cleanse, heal, purify, and sanctify them in every way. I was shown that as time goes on, people will only be able to survive both spiritually and physically through their faith and trust in God.

Some Will Watch Over Church Properties

Not every faithful Church member will head for the hills, so to speak. I was shown that some Saints will be asked to stay behind to take care of Temple Square, the Conference Center, and the surrounding Church buildings. Throughout the nation, faithful Saints will stay behind to watch over other temples, meetinghouses, Church-owned farms, and so on.

I was also shown there will be another location provided outside of the Salt Lake area for the gathering of the First Presidency and many of the other General Authorities of the LDS Church. From this location they will be able to continue to conduct Church business, and they will be provided for and protected. They will be able to continue and complete their missions in life.

There will come a time when the ability to communicate between Church leaders and camps becomes difficult. However, through the Spirit we will be able to communicate effectively and efficiently. We will be given aid and protection from those on the other side of the veil. Many of us will encounter and interact not only with spirit beings, but with translated and resurrected beings as well.

These messengers will aid us in every way. They will fortify our camps. They will help in communications. They will instruct us. They will lead us and intervene in our behalf. They will go before us, guiding us and teaching us as the Spirit directs.

The LDS-based film *17 Miracles* tells the story of the Willie and Martin handcart companies in 1856. Those Saints suffered greatly during their journey to Utah, but they also witnessed divine intervention in their behalf. The film gives clear examples of some of the miracles—and others like them—that will be experienced in the camps in our day. I was shown that in many cases we will experience similar circumstances and more, including miracles specifically mentioned in each book of scripture. We will experience those trials, adversities and miracles as well.

Through our faith, we will come to know our God. Through our faith, we will be cleansed, purified, and sanctified. Through the power of the Atonement of Jesus Christ, these things will be made possible. Through our faith, we will endure the "refiner's fire" and we will learn to become a Zion people. From these experiences, we will learn to trust the Lord in all things, and He will prepare us for our Savior's return.

CHAPTER NINE

Daily Life in the Three Types of Camps

Some have asked, "What will an average day in a camp be like?" In response, I will pose another question that has been asked: "What is the difference between a tent city, a Place of Refuge, and a City of Light?"

To clarify the difference between these three types of camps, let me explain a bit more. My understanding is that there will be thousands of tent cities all over the world. These will consist of people from all walks of life and from varying backgrounds.

Some tent cities will be established by various religious institutions. Some will be organized by individuals who have gathered together on their own for their own safety and welfare. Others will be organized by families who have joined together for safety in numbers. These I refer to as "tent cities."

When I refer to Places of Refuge, I am specifically talking about the camps that are planned and organized by the Church of Jesus Christ of Latter-day Saints. These are the camps that consist mainly of active members of this church, although there are some who join with them who are not of this faith. These are the camps I have referred to when discussing the gathering of the Saints once the invitation to gather has been given by Church leadership.

Again, this gathering will come as an invitation from the First Presidency of the Church, and not from any other source.

When I discuss Cities of Light, I am talking about camps that begin as Places of Refuge but that later become Cities of Light due to the faithfulness of the Saints. In these camps I have seen that there will be large tent tabernacles similar to those in the days of Moses, although modified for modern temple worship.

These Cities of Light are set up to prepare the Lord's people for the Second Coming of our Lord and Savior Jesus Christ. These Cities of Light are called such because the light of Christ will shine brightly from these camps. These places will be shielded and protected from the adversary because the faith of the people is so strong that the enemies of the Lord will not be able to penetrate their barriers.

Those in tent cities and particularly in Places of Refuge will also experience great protection and mighty miracles, based upon the faith of those within and without. Although great tragedy and suffering will still occur in these tent cities, the Lord will also pour out His tender mercies and many will be spared.

A Testing Ground

The Places of Refuge will serve as a testing ground. They will provide additional opportunities for learning and growth. They will provide safety in numbers and opportunities for individuals to learn to put aside the ways of the world. They will require selflessness and cooperation, and they will help many learn to serve and sacrifice. They will create an atmosphere of unity, strength, power and endurance. They will be the beginning of the "refiner's fire" in cleansing, purifying, uplifting, edifying and unifying God's children.

I view a "City of Light" as the final preparatory ground for sanctification and edification prior to the rebuilding of the stakes of Zion and the building of the New Jerusalem. During this time, there will be many who will experience an outpouring of the Spirit. Spiritual gifts will abound and will be magnified. Priesthood power will be strengthened tremendously. The faith of the people will be so great that some will become translated beings. Angels, translated and resurrected beings will visit and assist the people.

I was shown that surrounding many of the camps there were shields of protection. I saw that in some cases there were literal dome-like energy shields that had been placed over them. My understanding is that these "force fields" were put in place and activated by the faith of the people on both sides of the veil.

It is my understanding that during the time the Lord's people are being prepared in "Cities of Light," toward the end of the days of tribulations, many more of the 144,000 will begin to be called and set apart. Prior to the Lord's return, these missionaries will be sent out across the world to gather in the Lord's elect. These individuals will actively work to gather together those who have been lost and separated from the fold.

Water and Electricity

Some have asked, "Will we have running water and electricity in the camps?" and "Will an electromagnetic pulse (EMP) be used against America?"

My answer to these questions is that I believe there will be some water and electricity in at least some of the camps for some of the time. I really don't know for sure. I have been shown various scenes, but I do not have clear recollection on this subject. I do know that at some point in time, my family will be living in a camp without any running water and without electricity.

As I have prayed for greater clarity and understanding, the Spirit has born witness to me that for many there will be some modern conveniences for a time, and for others not necessarily so. There are just too many varying circumstances for me to be able to go into greater detail on this particular subject.

Each time I have petitioned the Lord to ask Him what I should share pertaining to this topic, the Spirit has born witness to me in reminding me of some of the other things the Lord has shown me. I have been reminded of the promptings my husband and I have been given regarding our physical preparations. We have been instructed to purchase several types of heat, light, and cooking sources. We have been instructed to get basic survival gear that would be needed in the event we have no electrical power and no running water.

Life in the Camp

I saw myself cooking over an open campfire. I saw us using Dutch ovens and other items. I saw myself hanging wet clothes outside on a clothesline hung between trees. I witnessed children playing in the summer breeze and people huddled closely around a warm campfire after a winter storm.

I saw a few people gardening, although I could not see what they had planted. I was shown scenes of dozens of tents grouped together in close proximity. I saw that these individuals worked together for their care and survival. I watched them care for their families and for each other.

I saw that some camps consisted of a hundred or more people, and in other tent cities I saw several hundred to thousands of people gathered together for safety and protection.

I witnessed men on horseback carrying supplies into the camps. I witnessed men on horseback scouting the areas and doing all they could to ensure the safety of the camps. I saw my husband mount a horse, carrying a rifle in one hand and guiding the horse with the other. It was made known to me that he was on guard duty and that he and many other men were stationed at various posts throughout and around the perimeters of the camp.

In another scene I saw my husband perched high up in a tree on "look out" for possible intruders. I was shown a few different scenes where I saw him and others out hunting for food. I saw him using his rifle, shotgun and bows for hunting.

I saw myself and several other women attending to the care and teaching of children. I saw that education continued in the camps and that it continued to be an important part of our lives. I saw us reading books, singing hymns and Primary songs, as well as other songs. I saw us dancing.

I saw us gathered around the campfire as families, singing, talking and playing. Some had brought portable musical instruments with them, and I saw that we very much enjoyed the music in the camps. I specifically remember a man playing an acoustic guitar, a woman playing a violin, and a child playing a flute. I remember hearing people playing harmonicas.

I saw children laughing and playing together, running throughout the camps playing games with one another. I also saw men, women and children working very hard to obtain firewood, water, food and other essential items. I saw people using some of their own supplies, as well as sharing with others in need.

I was shown examples of some of the assignments or jobs people had in the camps. Some of these assignments included camp set-up and organization, food preparation, sanitation duties, medical care, education, alternative health care, priesthood duties, gardening, sewing and mending of clothing, shoes and other items, gathering of firewood and other necessary supplies, and various other duties, including leadership roles.

It was made clear to me that the camps which were set up by the Church were organized in wards made up of families that consisted of approximately ten families per group. Designated priesthood leaders were assigned as captains of 10, 50 or 100. It was very organized and orderly.

I saw a few pets, but was not given specific information regarding this topic and who had brought animals or why. I did see a few scenes that included beehives, cows, chickens and other animals. A few of the larger dogs that I witnessed were being used as guard dogs or hunting dogs.

I was not told or shown how it was decided what animals were brought to the camps, and it was not made known to me what happened to the various pets of those who gathered to the Places of Refuge.

As I have mentioned, I saw that some of the camps had running water and other amenities for at least a period of time. Other camps seemed much more remote and isolated, and although it was made known to me that there were water sources nearby these camps, I got the feeling that the water had to be hauled in containers by hand into the actual camps.

I saw that most of the camps required that the water for drinking, cooking and in some cases bathing had to be purified. This was due to various causes, including but not limited to bacterial, fungal, or viral pathogens, as well as some biological chemical contamination.

I witnessed a few scenes where we were quarantined in our tents for extended periods of time due to various threats. I saw that we endured extremely cold temperatures, rain, sleet, hail, and ice and snow storms. I witnessed us enduring extreme heat, high winds, pestilence and other plaguing conditions.

I saw a few RVs, trailers, and motor homes in some of the camps. However, I was shown that for the most part, these were being used as little makeshift hospitals. It appeared to me that in most cases, these vehicles and trailers were being utilized for the elderly, the sick and infirm, pregnant women, new mothers, and small infants.

I watched families praying together and reading scriptures

together. I witnessed the Saints holding meetings where they worshipped together, prayed together, and fasted together.

I saw several people writing in journals, keeping records, and writing about their feelings, testimonies, and experiences in the camps. I witnessed the faith of hundreds being severely tested as the trials and adversities seemed endless.

I witnessed miraculous healings, babies being born, deaths, and in some cases, people being raised from the dead. I felt the joy, the sorrow, the pain, the faith, and the healing of those in the camps. It was made known to me again that everything I was being shown was part of God's eternal plan, and that He was over all.

I saw that my husband and I did not look much older than we do today. My dark hair was still dark. My husband's hair was still dark brown. I saw that my children did not look much older than they do today.

I saw that there were people of all ages in the camps. I saw families with babies and small children. I saw elderly people and single people. I noticed young teenage boys and girls. I was shown that there were pregnant women and new mothers and babies, young married couples, and people of varying backgrounds and cultures.

I saw that we had several types of sleeping bags—including those for warmer days, and those for snow and very cold freezing temperatures. I saw us camping in the rain, sleet, snow and high winds. I saw us camping in the fall, winter, spring and summer. I saw us camping in severe heat in bright sunshine, as well as in the dark.

I saw camps all over the world, although most of the camps I was shown were in the United States. I saw people coming from all over the United States, going to various camps. I saw that people gathered in many locations, and that the LDS Church had prepared places of safety for people all over the country. Some of these places included a few camps in the Northeast, Florida, Kansas, Missouri, Iowa, and other "stop off and rest locations" throughout the Midwest and western United States.

I was specifically shown that many people from the Eastern states were directed to go westward. As I have mentioned, I was shown that the Kansas City area was one of many places where those traveling stopped to rest and recuperate before continuing on their journey to their assigned camps.

Many people from California will seek refuge and safety in Arizona, Nevada and Utah. There will be some Places of Refuge in Arizona, but not many. However, Arizona has some very sacred places, and there will be increased efforts to work with the Native Americans there. They will play a key role in the events leading to the building of the New Jerusalem.

Cities of Light

Most of the Cities of Light I was shown were located in the Rocky Mountains. As I mentioned in *A Greater Tomorrow*, I was first shown these Cities of Light from an aerial view high in the sky as if from outer space. The sky was entirely dark. It was as if the entire earth was pitch black, with the exception of what at first appeared to be random specks of light scattered across the world. I was told that these specks of light were Cities of Light.

As I was shown these things from the sky, it was as if we then zoomed in on things and I was shown things in greater detail and up close. After seeing things from far away in the sky, we went toward North America, and then finally approached the United States. We hovered above the U.S. as I was shown and taught more.

After awhile, it was as if I were given a close-up view of some of these camps, with a focus given on the Cities of Light. I was taught about these future places. The purpose of these camps was explained to me. I was shown various examples of things which furthered my understanding of the Cities of Light.

Upon witnessing these Cities of Light, some of the many questions I asked were essentially, "What is this I am seeing?" "Why is everything so dark?" "Where is everyone?" "What is going on?"

One specific question I remember asking pertained to the darkness I was seeing and the little specks of light in the earth far in the distance. I asked, "Is the earth in total darkness?" The answer was yes. Then I asked, "Is this literal or figurative?" The answer I was given was, "Both."

When I inquired further, it was explained to me that what I was being shown was that in the last days prior to the Lord's return, there will be Cities of Light that will shine forth in the darkness that covers the earth. At this time, the earth will be dark due to a lack of physical light as well as spiritual light.

It was made clear to me that although there was great darkness upon the earth, the light could still be seen and was shining brightly upon the earth. I was given the understanding that this was both literal and symbolic.

Camps Across the World

There will be these three types of camps throughout the world, wherever there are stakes of Zion. The Church leaders have counseled members to stay in their countries, and there is wisdom in following that guidance. The main message the Lord wants me to convey is that we need to focus on being obedient and worthy, no matter where we live.

We must have the Spirit with us so we know what we need to do to prepare. Then we will know where we are supposed to be as we prepare for the Savior's Second Coming.

CHAPTER TEN

Natural Disasters Across the Earth

There is a misunderstanding by some who believe that the faithful Saints will be spared the calamities and trials that will come upon the world before the New Jerusalem is built and the Savior returns.

While it is important to have a positive outlook and know that God does protect the righteous, it is also important to recognize that protection comes in many ways. In some cases, protection comes in ways that we do not see. We must realize that sometimes the very trials we go through actually serve as forms of protection and often prepare us for other things which are to come.

Be aware that just because we are promised protection that does not mean we will avoid suffering. The Lord has not promised us that He will spare us of all trials and tribulations. He has promised us that He will give us the power and strength to overcome the adversary.

Through our faithful obedience to His commandments, we will be guided and directed by the Holy Ghost to know what to do, when to do it, and how to do it. He has promised us that He will not give us more than we can handle without providing a way to escape.

We have been taught in the scriptures that as part of our experience in mortality, we will be tried and tested. The Lord has promised us refuge from the storm, strength in the whirlwinds, and the ability to withstand the fiery darts of the adversary.

God has not promised that if we are righteous we will not struggle or that we will never get sick. He has not promised us that if we are righteous, our loved ones will not be maimed or even lose their lives. In fact, the opposite holds true.

We have been told that the more righteous we become, the more we will experience the fiery darts of the adversary. We have even been told that in some cases, the righteous will be called upon to give up their very lives for the sake of Zion.

We have been promised that God will not abandon us. No matter the sacrifices, no matter the suffering, no matter the heartaches and disappointments—it is worth it. We have been promised that if we do our part, if we repent, and if we do all in our power to apply the Atonement in our lives, we will one day be able to return and live with our loving Father in Heaven and receive the promised blessings of eternity.

We have been counseled to assume a wholesome and affirmative stance toward national and world conditions. We have been counseled to stand in holy places; to be counted worthy; to do all in our power to defend righteous principles; to do all we can to do our part in building the Kingdom of God on the earth. In the end however, what will be, will be.

The words of the prophets have never suggested that the world will get better as the Second Coming approaches. They have not taught that everyone will suddenly (or even gradually) begin to keep the commandments and eventually start to incorporate the teachings of Jesus Christ into their lives. They speak of quite a different picture.

President Joseph Fielding Smith taught, "It would be a sorry day for any nation, where the gospel is being preached, to drive the elders of the Church from its borders and deny them the right to preach the gospel among the people. The elders insure peace unto the nations, so long as they will hear the message of salvation and will protect and defend the truth. When the time comes that the nation will cast the elders out and no longer receive their testimony, woe be unto them.

"We read in the word of the Lord that after the testimony of the elders will come wrath and indignation upon the people. For after their testimony will come the testimony of earthquakes, that shall cause suffering and sorrow and men shall fall upon the ground for fear. There shall come also the testimony of thunderings, and the voice of lightnings, and the voice of tempests, and the voice of the waves of the sea heaving themselves beyond their bounds. All things shall be in commotion and men's hearts shall fail them because of fear that shall come upon the people. These things shall follow the testimony of the elders of the Church of Jesus Christ of Latter-day Saints, when the people of the world reject them and drive them from their borders." (*Doctrines of Salvation*, Vol. 3, pp. 7-8)

Our prophets and apostles have testified that all who stay on the gospel path will know the protection that comes only through faithfulness. They have testified of the difficulties that lie at our very doorsteps. They have warned us repeatedly of the need for us to prepare for the days of tribulation. They have explained that the righteous will experience many tender mercies from the Lord. They have testified that great miracles will occur.

The Prophet Joseph explained, however, that "it is a false idea that the Saints will escape all the judgments, whilst the wicked suffer; for all flesh is subject to suffer. ... Yet many of the righteous shall fall a prey to disease, to pestilence, etc. ... So that it is an unhallowed principle to say that such and such have transgressed because they have been preyed upon by disease or death, for all flesh is subject to death." (*History of the Church*, 4:11)

Keeping this in mind, I must admit it is quite sobering for me to write the next few chapters. In all honesty, I wish I could skip over this section and just focus on the beauty that lies ahead. I wish I could fast forward the clock and skip some of what must take place between now and the building of the New Jerusalem.

I say this in part because I know some of what I must do to prepare for that day. I would rather focus on all of the fun and uplifting aspects of the Last Days, rather than on the difficult days of destruction and cleansing that will surely come to pass.

I don't like to describe the negative in detail because I find it depressing to be reminded of the terrible things I have witnessed. I wish it were not so, because it isn't pleasant to think about what many of us will be called upon to endure. But "to be forewarned is to be forearmed" and this concept gives me reason to offer my witness to those who will hear it.

I do know that I am to write these things. I am to serve as a witness and an additional voice of warning to my brothers and sisters. I have been asked to write and speak the truths that I know, and in so doing, serve our Father's children by helping them open their hearts and minds to the Lord's message.

Sharing Additional Details

Some have asked for additional details about what I have been shown regarding specific areas of the country as well as of things in other lands. As I have pondered and prayed about this topic, I have struggled to know what it is the Lord would have me share. I know I was shown these things for several reasons, but most of what I was shown was intended just for me so that I could accomplish the mission the Lord has given me.

I am not going to spend much time and energy focusing on the details pertaining to the natural disasters and destructions, but I will share a small portion of what I feel the Lord wants me to share. I seek to get my points across and to be able to adequately express what needs to be said without creating undo fear and anxiety in those who read these words.

The Lord has been very specific with me that I need to tread lightly in this area. He does not want me or anyone else focusing on the doom and gloom, causing fear and panic. However, He does want us to wake up and get our houses in order, and to be able to do so out of faith and obedience, not out of fear.

The adversary is the one who wants us to fear. He is the one who wants us to get all worked up over the coming calamities. He is trying to paralyze us and keep us from acting. He is the master manipulator and another one of his tricks is to create mirages. He goes to great lengths to try to fool us into either becoming so afraid that we essentially go into shock, or he tries to lull us into a false sense of reality to dull our minds and hearts to keep us from seeing, feeling, and sensing what is really going on around us.

We must remember that although there is a veil that has been placed over mortal minds, there is no veil for Satan and those who work with him. They are very much aware of what is going on, who we are, and what is going to happen. They are anxiously awaiting the day when they can unleash their full power and utilize all of their forces. Those who are of the dark have and will continue to infiltrate and seek to overthrow the righteous. We know, however, that their efforts are in vain.

Where Are You in Life?

Before getting into any more detail regarding specific scenes I have been shown, I want to emphasize a few critical points. First, I want to encourage you to sit back and take an inventory of how you feel right now. Take a moment to think about who you are, what you are currently doing in your life, and where you think you are going.

I would ask that you take at least a few moments to reflect on your relationship with the Savior. Spend some time pondering and praying about the messages which have been shared in this book, the scriptures and other sources. Pray for clarity and understanding, and if impressed to do so, spend some time contemplating what you feel the Lord's plan is for you.

Listen. Wait. Ponder. Pray. Try to picture yourself now and in the future, and see if you can discern how the Spirit is speaking to you as an individual.

Learning to discern when and how the Lord speaks to us is critical. Learning, knowing and understanding when the Holy Ghost is speaking to us is essential to our salvation, and being able to discern the light from the dark in every aspect of our lives will be of great importance.

One day our ability to be able to do this will in fact be a matter of both life and death in every sense of the word—speaking both temporally and spiritually. Can you tell the difference between your own voice, the voice of the Lord, and the voice of the adversary? How do you know?

I ask you to pause here and reflect on what I'm asking you to do. These are simple questions but they deserve much consideration by us all. It is important to orient ourselves to better develop the skills of thinking and feeling. I encourage you to take the time and make the effort to learn and to develop the critical skill of discerning the Lord's voice.

The Lord's timing is always perfect. His ways are not our ways and because He knows all, we can put our faith and trust in Him and in what He tells us. So when we learn of things to come, good or ill, we can know for ourselves that it is all part of God's plan for us here on the earth.

The Earth is Ready for a Cleansing

As I mentioned in my first book, *A Greater Tomorrow*, the earth is tired and is weighed down by the sins of the world. The earth is getting ready and is waiting and wanting to be cleansed and purified. One of the many ways this cleansing will take place is through natural disasters.

Major upheavals of land and water help with this process. Much of the reason we have seen an increase in natural disasters over the past decades is because of this very thing. As time goes on, we will see and feel significant changes in the earth's energy.

Some of you may have seen some of the recent disaster movies, such as *2012*. Some of the action scenes were definitely over the top. Unfortunately, Hollywood's filmmakers are fairly accurate in some of their depictions of what awaits our country.

The time is fast approaching when those who choose not to heed the Prophet's invitation to gather will witness destruction on an unimaginable scale. I emphasize again that these scenes will happen after the Saints and other righteous people have gathered together in tent cities and Places of Refuge.

As I mentioned, I would much rather skip this chapter, but I know it is important to share these events. I hope these depictions will help others see the reality of what is coming. I mainly touch on larger cities, but please be aware that nearly every city or town across the earth will be affected.

These events will not all begin the same day or week, but it will feel like a chain reaction as the natural disasters seem to come in waves to a battered nation.

The American Northwest

I saw the so-called Ring of Fire come alive throughout the Pacific Ocean basin, and volcanic eruptions occurred that exceeded the 1980 explosion of Mount St. Helens. The states of

Washington, Oregon, and California were greatly affected. I also saw volcanoes in Southwestern states such as Arizona and New Mexico. Major earthquakes struck up and down both coasts of the United States at this time, as well as in Canada and throughout Central and South America.

I saw Seattle, Washington destroyed by volcanic eruptions, tsunamis, earthquakes, and fires. Tall buildings collapsed, unable to withstand the shaking and flooding. The Space Needle was destroyed. Lakes and ponds were flooded and contaminated. Many ferries capsized and were submerged underwater. The roads were broken up, and people could no longer travel from Seattle to British Columbia. In fact, most of Washington state was in ruins.

I saw people fleeing on foot, sometimes even barefoot with nothing but the clothes they were wearing or maybe a small backpack. They carried their infants and children in their arms, trying to flee to safety.

Huge forest fires raged. I saw similar things in Portland, Oregon, but for whatever reason I saw more intensity in Washington.

San Francisco

San Francisco was hit very hard. The entire region almost disappeared due to the worst earthquakes, and then the whole coast was flooded by terrible tsunamis that left many cities completely destroyed.

San Francisco Bay was unrecognizable. The Bay Bridge was torn in pieces and half of it fell into the ocean. The Golden Gate Bridge suffered a similar fate.

Cars, trucks, and trolley cars were thrown around like toys. The entire road system was torn apart. The steep streets had massive cracks in the earth and huge sinkholes where the vehicles just disappeared. They fell into the earth and were covered by debris. Skyscrapers crashed to the ground, and homes crumbled into rubble in what seemed a matter of minutes.

Hundreds of buildings fell into massive cracks or were buried by landslides. The entire region was demolished and there were very few survivors. The entire San Francisco Peninsula was cut off from the mainland and covered in water. Major tunnels were flooded, and the water system was contaminated and polluted. Most areas were without clean water and electricity.

The nearby city of Oakland suffered the same fate. The freeways were torn up and completely impassable, leaving people stranded and desperate. Within hours there were roving mobs and gangs ruling the streets. Fires were rampant throughout the region, and the California redwood forest was burning.

Los Angeles

Los Angeles and most of Southern California was also ravaged by earthquakes, tsunamis, and other natural disasters.

It was as if every Tinseltown movie was rolled into one, even down to the famous Hollywood sign falling apart and tumbling down the mountain.

Like many areas of the country, this area was hit with heavy rain and hail storms that caused major flooding, Massive fires still erupted, creating clouds of smoke that blanketed the city.

The story was the same all along the California, Oregon and Washington coasts. Gangs roamed the streets. Electrical grids were down, and most food and water was contaminated.

Earthquakes seemed to come one right after another, followed by tsunamis up and down the coasts.

Needless to say, the region's airports were shut down. The freeways were an impassible mess, and large bridges were ruined.

New York City

The destruction I saw in New York City was an example of what happened all along the East Coast. Skyscrapers and long-standing monuments crumbled into the pages of history.

Due to a series of earthquakes, tsunamis, and hurricanes, the cities in the greater New York metropolis area were so flooded that you could no longer recognize them. Lower Manhattan was under water, and pretty much all of Manhattan was uninhabitable. The famed skyline was decimated as fires spread from building to building. I saw that New York City's Central Park was "wiped clean" due to flooding. The glass panels of the United Nations Building were shattered.

At Coney Island, some parts of the amusement park attractions were scattered all over and I saw roller coaster pieces floating in the ocean. I saw people gathering at Yankee Stadium. It had been damaged, but people didn't know of anywhere else to go.

The transit system came to a standstill. The Brooklyn Bridge fell apart. Those people who survived the initial destruction were stranded in the city. Trains, subways, and ferries stopped completely. Tunnels were flooded and impassible, as were most roadways. Times Square became a death trap of violence and destruction.

Ellis Island was almost completely submerged and it was as if the upper half of the Statue of Liberty was floating in the water. Part of the torch had been bombed or otherwise destroyed. I don't remember exactly what caused that because it was a combination of things that all seemed to be happening at about the same time or one right after another.

Farther south, Washington D.C. was flooded and essentially abandoned. Florida was greatly affected on the coasts and people flocked to safety by trying to go inland, although they were battered by tropical storms.

I know it sounds inconceivable, but I saw volcanoes causing horrific destruction in Hawaii, Arizona, California, New Mexico, Washington, Oregon, Alaska, Wyoming, Montana, North Carolina, South Carolina, Virginia, Oklahoma and elsewhere.

These same issues were happening all over the country. Las Vegas was cut off from civilization when I-15 was damaged in both directions, and after the Hoover Dam cracked, they were soon out of water.

Along those lines, a major cause of the country's problems was that most of the dams across the country failed. This brought tremendous flooding, and caused hydroelectric plants throughout the country to go down, affecting the power grid.

Adding to the misery, the following winter brought freezing rains, ice, sleet, and hail and snow storms to most of the country.

Utah

Before the true destruction began, several minor earthquakes happened throughout the Mountain West. Then there was a fairly strong earthquake along the Wasatch Front that served to "wake people up" before the call to gather.

There was significant damage to key roadways and many homes, and landslides temporarily blocked some of the canyons. It made the national news, and there were many deaths reported, but the affected communities were able to repair things within a few weeks.

This earthquake helped inspire some people to get more prepared, but sadly, many others rejoiced that the "Big One" had finally come. They felt that "All is well in Zion" and even mocked those who dared say that something worse was still coming.

The prophet's invitation to gather came soon after this moderate earthquake. The faithful Saints left their homes and went to the Places of Refuge that had been prepared by the Church. Time passed, and some people in the camps got impatient and returned to their homes.

That was when a truly monstrous earthquake struck throughout Utah. The citizens in the Salt Lake Valley and Utah Valley were affected the most.

Unprecedented flooding occurred, with water coming up from the ground as well as numerous reservoir dams breaking in the canyons, sending walls of water racing into the cities below. Other major canyons were completely blocked off by thunderous landslides.

Downtown Salt Lake was absolutely slammed by the water, including Temple Square and the surrounding Church-owned buildings. Skyscrapers toppled, and the power was out everywhere. Fires began to rage all along the Wasatch Front, and the number of dead reached into the thousands.

Along the foothills, houses were shaken so badly that they slid right off the mountains or were buried by mudslides. The Point of the Mountain at the southern end of the Salt Lake Valley split almost in half, destroying I-15 and Redwood Road, making it impossible for anyone to cross through that area unless they made a treacherous hike around the destruction.

The Saints in the mountains at the Places of Refuge certainly got rocked, but the damage they faced was minimal in comparison. They put their tents and portable stoves back up and awaited word from the valleys.

Missouri

Some readers have asked about Brigham Young's prophecy that western Missouri will be swept clean before the Saints return there. That is true. I saw the whole area in shambles following a massive earthquake along the New Madrid Fault.

As I mentioned in *A Greater Tomorrow*, the earthquake

registered at least 9.0 on the Richter scale. It started in the Gulf of Mexico and reached St. Louis before splintering off into hundreds of smaller quakes.

The earthquake's true devastation was that it caused the Mississippi River, Missouri River and other waterways to temporarily reverse their courses, creating a huge tsunami that flooded all of Jackson County and the outlying areas. The Saints who currently live there will receive the prophet's invitation to gather to Places of Refuge that will keep them safe. If they follow him, I saw they would be spared the troubles that still must come to that area before the New Jerusalem is built.

Troubles Across the World

I was shown that the natural disasters occurred worldwide. It pains me to list these troubles, but I feel I must.

Every nation was affected. Some of the areas hit by volcanoes include: Philippines, Solomon Islands, Turkey, Greece, Indonesia, Japan, Costa Rica, Ecuador, Nicaragua, Chile, Russia, Guatemala, El Salvador, Fiji, Tonga and other islands in Polynesia, Iceland, Europe, Australia, New Zealand, Africa, Puerto Rico, Guam, and some in the Middle East—just to name a few.

Great Britain suffered flooding, fires, and severe storms. Buckingham Palace was destroyed, along with the Tower of London. I also saw castles throughout Europe destroyed.

In Australia, I saw the Sydney Opera House on fire. Denmark, the Netherlands and other countries received major destruction. The Panama Canal was flooded and contaminated. Cuba, Haiti, and the Dominican Republic were repeatedly blasted by hurricanes and tsunamis.

Even areas that avoided the hurricanes still faced tornadoes, strong winds, and massive rain and hail storms. Fires were seemingly always blazing throughout the cities, and the power grid became so unreliable that it was a surprise when the lights actually worked.

It Has Happened Before

People often express dismay that natural upheavals could happen so suddenly and powerfully. They cannot comprehend such destruction after so many centuries of relatively calm conditions.

All I can say is it has happened before. Nearly 2,000 years ago when Jesus Christ was crucified, the earth was racked with terrible convulsions. A giant earthquake hit Jerusalem, and other parts of the world were affected as well.

The Book of Mormon records the event in Third Nephi chapter 8. One day everything was calm, and then the next day everything literally crumbled. Verses 5 through 18 in particular parallel the same events that I have been describing.

Then in chapter 9, the Lord himself spoke from the heavens to the people and gave details of the destruction that had happened. In verse 12, He explained why it occurred: "And many great destructions have I caused to come upon this land, and upon this people, because of their wickedness and their abominations."

Then the Lord extended a hand of love and mercy in verse 13: "O all ye that are spared because ye were more righteous than they, will ye not now return unto me, and repent of your sins, and be converted, that I may heal you?"

He is offering the same loving opportunity to us. May we heed the words of the Lord's prophets today so that we will be spared the worst of what is to come.

CHAPTER ELEVEN

Plagues and Sicknesses

One of the most-often quoted scriptures concerning the Last Days is D&C 45:31, revealed to the Prophet Joseph Smith: "And there shall be men standing in that generation, that shall not pass until they shall see an overflowing scourge; for a desolating sickness shall cover the land."

Many readers have asked me if I saw something similar. The simplest answer is yes. Eventually there will be a huge pandemic. Actually, several different pandemics will occur.

Two years after receiving the above revelation, Joseph Smith said in 1833: "And now I am prepared to say by the authority of Jesus Christ, that not many years shall pass away before the United States shall present such a scene of bloodshed as has not a parallel in the history of our nation; pestilence, hail, famine, and earthquake will sweep the wicked of this generation from off the face of the land, to open and prepare the way for the return of the lost tribes of Israel from the north country." (*History of the Church,* 1:312-16)

That statement could scare the daylights out of anyone, but there is a glimmer of hope at the conclusion. The prophet is hinting that these scenes of turmoil have a purpose—to prepare the way for the return of the Ten Tribes and the building of the New Jerusalem.

Some Plagues Will Come Before the Gathering

The Saints won't be completely free from facing these plagues. Some of the plagues will start in various places prior to the gathering to Places of Safety. However, the most ominous and deadly plagues will come after we have been called to gather.

These plagues will reach some of the camps, but on a much smaller scale. We will be able to fight the plagues and other diseases while in the camps through a variety of healing methods. Faith will be the greatest weapon available. When medication either does not work or is not available, some will turn to alternative health care methods such as herbal remedies and essential oils. When those options run out or are unavailable, the Lord will provide other healing avenues for us. Ultimately however, it is the power of the priesthood and the faith of the people that will heal individuals through the Atonement of Jesus Christ. Some will be miraculously healed, while others will be called home to the other side of the veil to continue their work there.

Evil Powers Are At Work

I saw there are evil people actually working on creating these plagues, diseases, sicknesses and chemical weapons. They have already been working on developing these weapons for decades and in the past few years have started to unleash some of them on a very small scale. They will continue to do so with the ultimate goal to be in complete control and to have domination of the land and over the people.

One of their goals is to significantly decrease not only the population of the United States, but also the population of the world in general, thereby making it easier for them to usurp their power and control. They would also have less resistance from those who are unwilling to follow their orders, obey their demands, or give in to their threats.

I saw that some man-made biological weapons will be unleashed, along with some chemical weapons, and even some nuclear weapons. All three types will hit the United States.

Many people have asked me about the Ebola virus. There are many different strains of the Ebola virus. Most have been manufactured and purposefully mutated to cause the most harm possible and to keep people from being able to trace the origins or diagnose the proper treatment. It will continue to be a serious health problem throughout the world.

I have also seen a more serious plague that will eventually come to the U.S. This is the same one others have written about—the one that gives people purplish-colored, flesh-decaying spots starting on their hands and faces. This will come later on, though.

Beware of Plague Remedies

There have been and will continue to be individuals who claim they have solutions or remedies for fighting the plague. I was shown that in the next few years, more and more people will come forward making such claims. I was shown that for the most part, there are no actual cure-alls for the coming plagues. There will simply be too many types and strands out there to be able to effectively know how to combat them once exposed to them.

There will be many that are manufactured in labs and designed to resist and fight against the causes of the plagues, However, some of these "Plague Be Gone" formulas will do more damage than good. Many of them were inspired by the adversary to fool people into a false belief that they can administer this potion and be saved from a particular plague or disease.

In some cases, those who have manufactured and developed these plague-fighting formulas think they have been inspired by angels of the light, when in fact they have been given this information by those on the dark side masquerading and pretending to be angels of light. Not only will these formulas not work, they will actually have the opposite effect.

I was shown scenes of people in a panic who are afflicted. They ingest this formula, then they will take more and more as they get sicker and sicker, not realizing that the supposed healing remedy is actually doing them more harm and increasing the poisons and toxins in their bodies.

I have not researched this topic and really do not know who will develop these plague-fighting formulas, but I was specifically shown a few people and scenarios pertaining to this subject. I remember being warned very clearly to not partake of these substances and counseled not to administer them to others.

The feeling I was left with was that the name "Plague Be Gone" was symbolic in that it represented several different "concoctions" that would be marketed for this purpose. I was shown specific people to be aware of, and they were given to me as examples of what was to come.

Maybe "Plague Be Gone" is also literal in that someone has or will soon develop a product with this name. It will be interesting to see what happens over the next year or so.

Our only true safety from the plagues will be to follow the counsel of the living prophet by heeding the call and invitation to places of safety.

As I mentioned, the worst plagues in the United States will hit after the call to gather, so those that gather will be greatly protected. They will be separated out and in safe havens before the plagues hit the U.S. cities in dramatic fashion. While I have been shown that there will be some sickness and disease and even some plagues that hit the camps, it will be nothing compared to what happens in the outside world.

Miracles in the Camps

We will experience such amazing miracles in the Places of Refuge that there are not words to adequately describe what I have seen. In addition to the curing of disease, people will regain sight, hearing, the ability to walk again, and in some cases will be raised from the dead. Essentially all of the miracles testified of in the scriptures (and more) will be experienced in the camps.

Some will die of seemingly small things, while others will live and be healed from sickness and disease that seems sure to kill them. These healings will come most often from Priesthood blessings, but always because of the faith of the afflicted individual, along with the faith of friends and loved ones who were pleading and praying for the healing to occur.

Of course, ultimately the decision lies with the Lord, so those that are miraculously healed will realize it is the Lord's will that they continue to live. Their earthly mission is not yet complete.

Who Is Your Master?

We have to decide who our Master truly is. There will be no fence sitting as we move into the future. Either we will choose to follow the Lord's prophet, or we will choose otherwise and will be left on our own. This is no different than it is for us today—only the stakes will be much higher and the consequences that much greater. For many it will be a matter of life and death—both spiritually as well as temporally.

I choose to live. I choose to follow the true Master of all. I choose to listen to and follow the Lord's Prophet. I choose to put my trust and faith in God. I choose safety. I choose to do all I can to help myself, my family, my loved ones—and anyone else I can along the way—to heed the counsel and to discern truth.

In 2010, Elder Dallin H. Oaks gave a wonderful General Conference talk entitled "Healing the Sick."

Elder Oaks said, "The use of medical science is not at odds with our prayers of faith and our reliance on priesthood blessings. When a person requested a priesthood blessing, Brigham Young would ask, 'Have you used any remedies?' To those who said no because 'we wish the Elders to lay hands upon us, and we have faith that we shall be healed,' President Young replied: 'That is very inconsistent according to my faith. If we are sick, and ask the Lord to heal us, and to do all for us that is necessary to be done, according to my understanding of the Gospel of salvation, I might as well ask the Lord to cause my wheat and corn to grow, without my plowing the ground and casting in the seed. It appears consistent to me to apply every remedy that comes within the range of my knowledge, and [then] to ask my Father in Heaven... to sanctify that application to the healing of my body.'"

Elder Oaks added, "Of course we don't wait until all other methods are exhausted before we pray in faith or give priesthood blessings for healing. In emergencies, prayers and blessings come first. Most often we pursue all efforts simultaneously. This follows the scriptural teachings that we should 'pray always' (D&C 90:24) and that all things should be done in wisdom and order." *(Ensign,* April 2010)

I believe that this advice will hold true when we are confronted with the plague as well as many of the illnesses and trials of health we face today. We will need to do all within our range of knowledge, and utilize the gifts the Lord has given us, in addition to asking for and receiving healing through Priesthood blessings.

I believe the scriptures have given us very specific advice on avoiding the plagues of the last days in D&C 89:18-21:

"And all saints who remember to keep and do these sayings, walking in obedience to the commandments, shall receive health in their navel and marrow to their bones;

"And shall find wisdom and great treasures of knowledge, even hidden treasures;

"And shall run and not be weary, and shall walk and not faint.

"And I, the Lord, give unto them a promise, that the destroying angel shall pass by them, as the children of Israel, and not slay them. Amen."

The destroying angel that passed by the children of Israel and did not slay them was the plague. If we expect to enjoy this same blessing, I believe that we should take heed to the Lord's counsel in the Word of Wisdom. There is much more to this commandment than simply avoiding alcoholic beverages, tobacco use and "hot drinks."

Yes, we must rely on the Lord, but understand that usually the Lord will expect us to do all we can, and then through the power of the priesthood and divine intervention we can be healed—if it is His will.

I still struggle with many health issues, and yet I know I have been promised that one day I will be healed completely, while in the flesh, not as a resurrected being.

So my situation is not much different from those with other health issues. I need to have complete faith that what the Lord has promised will in fact happen. I will tell you honestly that right now my faith is not where it needs to be for this to happen. I do believe that gradually, if I keep doing the best I can to have faith and trust the Lord, I will in fact be able to "step up to the plate" and have the required faith when the time is right.

I do not remember being shown this during my NDE. This knowledge has come to me little by little over the years since my NDE as I have struggled with health challenges and as I have prayed, read my scriptures, and attended the temple.

I know that miraculous healing will occur for many people. I was shown this many times and I do have clarity on that. I am just still learning for myself how that will apply to my individual situation. I am on medication that according to doctors, I have to take. I know that the day will come when that medication will not be available. So my challenge, like so many others, is to have the faith required to go forward, to obey the Prophet when the call comes, and to put my faith and trust in His Eternal Plan for me.

I am no different than each of you. We all have our trials and struggles and each of us has been and will continue to be tried and tested, but I know that as we put our faith and trust in God, we will be fine. Whether we live through the upcoming tribulations or not, we will be where we are meant to be as it was designed in the Councils in Heaven before the world was. We are not innocent victims. We have choice and accountability, and we took an active part in designing our individual plan. We chose the lives we are living.

It has been made very clear to me that I am not just a victim of my health trials, or any other trial I have faced in my life. I chose them. Knowing this has changed my perspective on them and how I choose to act and feel about them.

Rather than feeling angry about them, I now feel grateful. They are actually a tender mercy from the Lord, and they are helping me develop my relationship with the Savior and with our Father in Heaven. They are helping me to become the woman that I am meant to become—the woman God knows I can be.

The same can be said concerning any health issues that may come in the future—no matter the source, no matter the cause, and no matter the outcome. What truly matters is what we choose to do, how we choose to react, and whether or not we are right with the Lord. In the end, whether we live or die, as long as we have solidified our testimonies and relationship with God and we have put our total and complete faith and trust in Him, we cannot go wrong.

CHAPTER TWELVE

---- ❧ ----

The U.S. Government Implements Martial Law

I saw that the combination of natural disasters and plagues sent the United States into an economic tailspin. The normal course of life was greatly disrupted. Many businesses shut their doors and never opened again. Food and other commodities became harder to obtain as supplies dwindled, sending prices skyrocketing.

American citizens were caught unprepared, and the tension in many cities led to riots and demonstrations, demanding that the U.S. Government take control of the situation. The country's leaders responded, using the country's economic struggles as an opportunity to fully implement "the chip."

The Use of Implanted Microchips

I was shown that the day is not far off when our world governments will implement the use of microchip implants on a very broad, yet personal scale. In actuality, some of this technology is already being utilized. Basic "introductory" chip implants have already been introduced to the public at large.

Various forms of the chip are being used on pets, zoo animals and others. Some people have already willingly submitted to the use of these devices, often not fully realizing the implications of their actions. Several people have been "required" to undergo procedures that have served as a "stepping stone" per say, to the devices that will be used in the future.

I have seen that increasingly so in the next few years, we will begin to hear and see more and more propaganda about the benefits of using the chip. I saw that those who were in power demanded the use of this technology more and more to the point that eventually they made it nearly impossible to buy, sell or trade anything without the use of the chip.

I saw that the government's initial invitation to get the chip was enticing, with benefits and rewards for those who participated willingly. However, I saw that those who held positions of power eventually threatened the lives of men, women, and children if they did not submit and comply with their demands. This technology was being used to track, trace, torture, and control the people.

I was also shown that there were many who refused to get the chip implants. They stood up against the masses in defense of their freedoms because they recognized the evils placed before them. I saw the unsettling result of standing up to the government as many people sacrificed their lives rather than receive the chip.

Troubles in Chicago

As part of these troubles, I was shown that the day will come when the great city of Chicago will lie in ruin. I was shown that the seeds of wickedness and corruption which were long ago planted in that city will soon ripen and lead to its very destruction. I was shown that civil unrest will increase immensely and soon the prophecies of past prophets and apostles will come to pass.

One such prophecy is that given by the Prophet Joseph Smith, as recorded in a letter written by Nephi Packard, a faithful member of the LDS Church. He wrote:

"My brother, Noah Packard, says that he heard the Prophet Joseph Smith say that the next great (U.S. civil) war after the war of the rebellion (the Civil War of the 1860s between the North and the South) would commence in a little town now called Chicago but at that time it would have grown to be a very large city. And another brother told me that the Prophet said that the cause of the next great trouble of the United States would be the depreciation of the currency of the United States." (*LDS Church Archives*, letter from Nephi Packard to A. Milton Musser, July 24, 1896)

I was shown that the start of this next civil war within the United States was mostly due to the planned and calculated attempts of conspiring men to start civil unrest through so-called "race riots." I was shown that within the city of Chicago there has been and will continue to be great effort made to create an atmosphere of chaos and fear.

I was shown that Chicago is the place that has been chosen as the "center stage" and the location for the "tipping point" of the events which these conspiring men and woman plan to use as their excuse to spread their messages of anger, hate and fear.

I saw that the Sears Tower (now renamed as the Willis Tower), was destroyed, along with several other buildings in the downtown area. I saw that monuments, museums and other historical buildings that are cherished were completely wiped out. I witnessed bombings, fires, roving gangs, and a variety of other wicked acts being performed. It was atrocious.

Martial Law Put Into Effect

I saw that prior to and during this time, Martial Law was declared across the nation as the economy collapsed. I witnessed some of the assassinations of prominent men and women as the evil forces consolidated their power.

The Saints living in the Places of Refuge were able to remain undetected for the most part as the government officials focused on controlling the citizens.

I saw people gathered by armed forces into sports stadiums, government buildings, schools, churches, FEMA camps, and other locations. I saw that families were purposely split up, dividing the women and the children from the men. Later, they divided the children from their mothers.

These wicked forces utilized public transportation, buses, trains, and other methods to accomplish their designs of transporting the people to what were essentially concentration camps, where I witnessed the use of chemical and biological weapons upon the masses, similar to the darkest days of World War II.

I was shown that although the fight will be difficult, those who stand for light and truth will be victorious. The wicked will not prevail in the long run. They will be stopped and the power of the Lord will overtake them.

Unfortunately, I was shown that the days of darkness were not over yet. War was coming to the United States.

CHAPTER THIRTEEN

Foreign Troops Arrive on U.S. Soil

I saw that during the turbulent period when the United States was under Martial Law, the country received assistance from the United Nations in an effort to get society back on track. Troops were sent to the larger cities to stop the rioting and other forms of violence.

However, there are already U.N. "peacekeeping troops" on U.S. soil. I saw that more will come. I saw that foreign troops from various nations rose up against the American people, seeking to take over the land.

I saw that at first many were somewhat complacent about the fact that there were foreign troops on our soil. I also saw that there were many others who were very upset about what was happening to our country, but they had trouble making their voices heard.

Russia and China Invade

Within a short time, I witnessed Russian and Chinese troops invading the U.S. coasts and then coming inland. I saw that there were also some North Korean troops assisting the Chinese. It was made known to me that Russia and China have been collaborating on their war strategies and planning this invasion ᴜᵢ ᴍany years. I was shown that their goal, along with that of other conspiring governments, is to try to eliminate millions of U.S. citizens along with much of our country's infrastructure, yet preserve as much of the land and cities as possible so that they can occupy it themselves.

I was shown that they also want to enslave the American people to the point that we are completely dependent on them for our welfare and survival. I saw foreign troops penetrate just about every region of our nation.

As I mentioned in *A Greater Tomorrow*, I was also shown that millions of people from countries in Central and South America will storm the southern border and will begin to take over much of the country, including a great part of Arizona.

I think this is an important detail, because during the Savior's visit to the American continent following His resurrection, He mentioned this occurrence. In Third Nephi 20:15-16 it reads:

"And I say unto you, that if the Gentiles do not repent after the blessing which they shall receive, after they have scattered my people——

"Then shall ye, who are a remnant of the house of Jacob, go forth among them; and ye shall be in the midst of them who shall be many; and ye shall be among them as a lion among the beasts of the forest, and as a young lion among the flocks of sheep, who, if he goeth through both treadeth down and teareth in pieces, and none can deliver."

The Savior later said in Third Nephi 21:12:

"And my people who are a remnant of Jacob shall be among the Gentiles, yea, in the midst of them as a lion among the beasts of the forest, as a young lion among the flocks of sheep, who, if he go through both treadeth down and teareth in pieces, and none can deliver."

The descendants of Lehi will be fulfilling Book of Mormon prophecies. As the American people turn their back on God, the nation will be torn up and occupied by these people. The current border crossings are a small trickle compared to what is to come.

What About an EMP?

Some people who have contacted me have wondered about electromagnetic pulse (EMP) bombs or devices being used in the future to knock out electronic equipment in the U.S.

As some may know, many devices including computers, controllers of various kinds, microwave ovens, electric clocks, automobiles, airplanes, guided missile defense systems, and so on might be rendered completely inactive and dysfunctional by such a bomb.

I have read from a few sources that a nuclear device such as those tested by the North Koreans can be modified to produce gamma rays instead of an explosion, then sent 30 miles up and exploded to incapacitate most electronic equipment in the U.S.

Many people who have also had dreams or visions have seen lots of vehicles stalled or abandoned on the roads and highways in the future. This could be due to a number of issues, including gasoline shortages or the inability to get new parts. It could also be due to the effects of natural disasters as well as various other wartime activities.

I have been asked several times whether I saw an actual EMP. My answer is that I do not have a clear recollection of this. As mentioned in a previous chapter, I was shown several night scenes from high above the earth. Upon being shown these scenes, I asked, "Is the whole earth dark?"

The answer was yes. I then asked, "Is this literal or figurative?" The answer was "both."

That is really all I know about this topic. I have inquired of the Lord further, but His answer continues to be that I just need to trust in Him and follow the Spirit. I was told I need to focus on what pertains to my family and me, and not get caught up in worrying about an EMP.

The Prophets Spoke About This War

As many are already aware, President John Taylor stated very clearly on several different occasions that the United States would have other nations come against her in war. I shared the following quote in the first chapter, but I want to emphasize it again.

President Taylor said, "Were we surprised when the last terrible war took place here in the United States? No. Good Latter-day Saints were not, for they had been told about it. Joseph Smith had told them where it would start in South Carolina. But I tell you today the end is not yet. You will see worse things than that, for God will lay his hand upon this nation, and they will feel it more terribly than even they have done before. There will be more bloodshed, more ruin, more devastation than ever they have seen before. Write it down! You will see it come to pass; it is only just starting in. And would you feel to rejoice? No; I would feel sorry. I knew very well myself when this last war was commencing and could have wept and did weep, over this nation; but there is yet to come a sound of war, trouble and distress, in which brother will be arrayed against brother, father against son, son against father, a scene of desolation and destruction that will permeate our land until it will be a vexation to hear the report thereof." (*Journal of Discourses*, Vol. 20:318, given on October 6, 1879)

Elder Orson Pratt of the Quorum of the Twelve Apostles also described the anarchy that would sweep the nation:

"What then will be the condition of that people, when this great and terrible war shall come? It will be very different from the war between the North and the South. Do you wish me to describe it? I will do so. It will be a war of neighborhood against neighborhood, city against city, county against county, state against state, and they will go forth destroying and being destroyed, and manufacturing will, in a great measure, cease, for a time, among the American nation.

"Why? Because in these terrible wars, they will not be privileged to manufacture; there will be too much bloodshed, too much mobocracy, too much going forth in bands and destroying and pillaging the land to suffer people to pursue any local vocation with any degree of safety.

"What will become of millions of the farmers upon that land? They will leave their farms and they will flee before the ravaging armies from place to place; and thus will they go forth burning and pillaging the whole country; and that great and powerful nation, will be wasted away, unless they repent." (*Journal of Discourses*, Vol. 20:151, given on March 9, 1879)

Many Witnesses

Many other people have been shown that foreign troops will invade the United States. Just in the past few months I have personally been contacted by literally hundreds of people attesting to this fact. What I have shared is just another witness of what we have already been told.

The foreign troops are coming and we need to be ready to do our part to stand for truth and righteousness. We need to be prepared for the days that will soon be upon us.

CHAPTER FOURTEEN

The Saints Gather into Larger Groups

As the terrible earthquakes, plagues and foreign invasions were happening, the Saints who had gathered to the Places of Refuge were anxiously awaiting answers. I was shown that there were limited forms of communication, such as ham radios, used between the camps. Also, members who had stayed behind in the valleys relayed information to Church leaders, so the Saints were somewhat aware of the destruction taking place. The descriptions they were receiving were almost unbelievable, and they wondered how anyone was surviving in the cities.

During this time, I saw the Saints gathered often in prayer. I saw that they were praying not only for their own protection, but also for those friends and relatives who had stayed behind in the valleys.

Enduring the Winter

The first winter was a challenge, especially in the high mountain camps where the snow was piled deep. This was a time of testing and refinement. Many faithful Saints with health problems who had still heeded the prophet didn't make it through the winter. It was always emotional to lose loved ones, but even on their deathbeds these Saints knew they were simply passing through the veil and would continue the Lord's work on the other side.

The winter had a refining effect on the Saints, and they became more selfless and focused on spiritual matters as memories of their previous materialistic lifestyle began to fade. It was helping them take steps toward becoming a Zion people.

I saw that the Saints in the Places of Refuge fared okay during the winter, but those people living in the tent cities suffered greatly due to a lack of preparation. The tent cities also were more easily located by the foreign troops, and many horrific things happened there.

The Canyons Are Closed Off

As I mentioned earlier, the earthquakes had closed off many of the major canyons with rockslides. The roads were buried or severely damaged, helping protect the Places of Refuge from the foreign troops and other marauders.

I was shown that after the roads and canyons were closed off through earthquakes, the Saints in the more spiritually refined camps received instructions to gather into larger groups in preparation for their next assignments. I specifically saw Cache Valley (Logan) and Sanpete County (Manti) as places where these larger groups congregated, but I was aware of several others.

This was a challenging undertaking for the Saints compared to the first round of gathering, when a lot of people arrived at the camps in vehicles or buses. This time it was done on foot along mountainous backroads and trails to avoid facing troublemakers from the valleys.

I was shown the leaders of the camps scouting out possible routes through the mountains to the gathering places. The camps soon hummed with activity as supplies were packed up. I saw people hastily create modern versions of handcarts and wagons by using parts from the now-useless cars and trucks.

Once the journey was underway, there were the usual mishaps and setbacks. Sometimes the journey took them several weeks, but it was a great relief to join with the other Saints. The spirit of unity and safety increased as the groups that had consisted of only dozens or hundreds of Saints now swelled to thousands in each camp.

The Purpose of the Larger Groups

I saw these larger groups preparing to perform great and marvelous works for the Lord once the destructions were over, including building Cities of Light throughout the land.

I mention this because there is a common misconception in the Church that before Christ returns in glory, all of the faithful Saints will be asked to move to Independence, Missouri and build the New Jerusalem. This is not entirely correct.

Yes, some of the faithful Saints will be assigned to build the New Jerusalem, but not everyone will be called to go to Missouri and the surrounding areas. I saw other groups building other Cities of Light or even returning to their previous areas to rebuild them once the wicked had departed or were destroyed.

The Lord will utilize the talents and gifts of His people wherever and however He deems appropriate. This applies to the building of the Center Stake of Zion as well as other locations around the world.

I saw that some will be asked to build temples, while others will be asked to help build homes and schools. Some will be given the assignment of planting gardens and tilling the ground for harvest.

I saw that the New Jerusalem and the other Cities of Light will be built by mortal beings as well as translated, resurrected and angelic beings.

Many people will be called to other places throughout the world to build and strengthen those areas. These assignments were foreordained. Things are not coincidental and do not just occur randomly or by happenstance. Where we end up and how we get there is all part of God's great eternal plan. It is up to us to choose to do our part and fulfill the measure of our creation.

As true servants of the Lord, we are to wait patiently upon the Lord in all things. We should not "run before we are sent" nor should we "run before our leaders."

Of course, we are to do all we can to listen to and follow the direction of the Spirit, so in several cases there are members who have already been or will be called to go to various places to prepare for the many events that are to come.

When the right time comes for us, we will be given further directions through the Lord's prophet, who will instruct us in what we need to do, where we need to go, and how we are to gather.

CHAPTER FIFTEEN

The Elders of Israel Defend Their Liberty

There was another purpose for gathering the Saints into larger groups—to regain our liberty. As has been prophesied in scripture, the day will soon come when we will be called upon as a people to stand for truth and liberty.

Many of us will be asked to sacrifice all that we have. Some will be asked to give of their lives in defense of the very principles we believe in and live by.

As the Saints settled into the larger camps, I saw nearly a year had passed since the United States had been invaded by foreign troops. These armies had caused great destruction and were on the verge of finishing their task of conquering the nation.

There were still pockets of opposition in certain parts of the country, but for the most part, it looked like the war was over. The "Land of the Free" was close to falling completely into evil hands.

At this crucial moment, the Lord called upon his righteous servants in the camps to defend their freedoms. The Elders of Israel were asked to fight for their religious freedoms, their lands, and their people. I saw men of all ages respond to fight for this cause.

My Own Family Will Fight for Truth

I was shown that my husband, my son and many other family members decided to heed this call. I was left with a clear recollection of these circumstances, and they have weighed heavily on my heart for more than ten years now.

In fervent prayer I have asked the Lord many times if this truly must be. His answer is always the same. He has confirmed the truth of this message and He has brought me comfort. As I have poured my heart out to God, He has continued to remind me of His Plan. He has continued to teach me to have greater faith and understanding.

He has reminded me that although I will lose some of my loved ones in this battle, we will not be separated for long. He has reminded me that those who were foreordained for this mission in the premortal life will be blessed for their sacrifice and service. He has reminded me that the very ones I will lose in mortality will also be some of those who will help me to continue and successfully complete my earthly mission from the other side of the veil.

Comparable to the 2,000 Stripling Warriors

The Lord has also often reminded me of the story in the Book of Mormon about the 2,000 Stripling Warriors. I have been shown that like these 2,000 Stripling Warriors, many of our young men will return to us alive and well. We will experience similar miracles and incredible divine interventions.

I have been shown that our loved ones who are fighting for righteousness will often be guided and protected by those on the other side of the veil. I have been shown that many of our men will return unharmed, telling of tender mercies and miraculous circumstances almost beyond belief.

I do not have full clarity how the war ended, but in a

miraculous way—through the efforts of the Elders of Israel and the hand of the Lord—the enemy was vanquished from the land. We all rejoiced, hardly able to believe that our years of struggle and problems were coming to an end. The time had finally come to establish Zion.

Once the major battle was over in the United States, the establishment of the Cities of Light moved into full operation. New Jerusalem was officially established, and work began on the magnificent temple that would be the centerpiece of Zion.

The areas near the previously built temples throughout the country were among the first areas to be repopulated by the Saints. The talents and skills of Church members made it possible to get the electrical plants running again.

Several groups returned to the damaged cities of Utah's Wasatch Front and began the rebuilding process there. I saw that having the temples become fully operational again was a key priority, along with resuming family history research so that ordinance work could be performed for those who had passed on.

I saw that the Church had wisely digitally preserved the previous temple records, and it wasn't long before temple work was being completed at a faster rate than ever before.

Missionaries Are Called Once Again

As the war ended, there were still millions of non-LDS citizens across the United States who had survived, either in tent cities or simply on their own. They had been deeply humbled by the horrors they had witnessed, and they were now much more receptive to the gospel message. I saw that thousands of Saints were called on missions to various lands, including official calls to 144,000 missionaries. Through these missionary efforts, millions of people eventually joined the Church and contributed their talents to building the Kingdom of God.

Some of the nation's major cities would never be fully rebuilt, and some were simply left desolate, including Washington D.C. However, I saw that eventually the United States of America once again became a promised land. A tremendous capital city was being built in the center of the country—the New Jerusalem.

CHAPTER SIXTEEN

———— ❧ ————

Life in New Jerusalem

In *A Greater Tomorrow*, I went into detail about many aspects of life in the New Jerusalem, but I felt prompted to give additional information. Many prophets and apostles have seen the city in vision, and I have included their quotations in this chapter to help describe the beauty and peace that I saw there.

Prophetic Words about New Jerusalem

Elder George Q. Cannon said: "We appreciate the home that God has given here (in Utah), which is so fruitful in blessings to the Saints; but we look forward to that land with indescribable feelings, because it is the place where God has said His city shall be built." (*Journal of Discourses*, Vol. 11:336-337, given on March 3, 1867)

Orson Pratt said this about the construction of the New Jerusalem: "Suffice it to say that God by revelation will inspire his servants and will dictate to them the order of the buildings of that city—the number and width of the streets, the kind of homes, the character of the Temple that is to be built therein, the kind of rock, timber and the various material that will have to be brought from a distance to enter into the composition of that beautiful city." (*Journal of Discourses*, Vol. 15:365, given on March 9, 1873)

President John Taylor said the following: "We talk of returning to Jackson County to build the most magnificent temple that ever was formed on the earth and the most splendid city that was ever erected; yea, cities, if you please. The architectural designs of those splendid edifices, cities, walls, gardens, bowers, streets, etc., will be under the direction of the Lord, who will control and manage all those matters; and the people, from the President down, will be under the guidance and direction of the Lord in all the pursuits of human life." (*Journal of Discourses*, Vol. 10:148, given on April 6, 1863)

In the same speech, President Taylor also taught, "We shall rear splendid edifices, magnificent temples and beautiful cities that shall become the pride, praise and glory of the whole earth. We believe that this people will excel in literature, in science and the arts and in manufactures, and be the most healthy and the most intellectual people that will reside upon the earth. This is part and parcel of our faith; in fact, Zion will become the praise of the whole earth." (*Journal of Discourses*, Vol. 10:148, given on April 6, 1863)

Elder Orson Pratt spoke of the varied activities that will take place in the New Jerusalem. He said, "Perhaps you may still further inquire concerning our emigration to the eastern boundaries of the State of Kansas, and to the western boundaries of the State of Missouri, what we intend to do in that part of the country? We expect to be farmers, a great many of us. We expect to introduce all kinds of machinery and manufactures. We expect to build mills. We expect to become a very industrious, frugal, economical people. We expect to have our merchandise and our stores and storehouses in that land. We expect to build a great many hundred schoolhouses in that country. We do not calculate to neglect our children in regard to their education. We expect to erect universities for the still higher branches to be taught. We expect to build many hundreds of meetinghouses, and we expect to be a people very densely located there—not one man taking up six or eight miles of land and calling it his farm; we don't expect to live that way, but we expect to settle a very dense settlement in that region." (*Journal of Discourses*, Vol. 24:23, given on October 26, 1879)

I testify of these same things. New Jerusalem will be everything that we can possibly imagine, and more.

The Living Water

Several people have asked me questions about "The Living Water." In my first book I briefly discussed this topic. I talked about when I was in the Spirit World I saw actual water with special properties. A few people have asked me, "Is this water found on earth as well?"

My simple answer is yes. There is and will continue to be Living Water found upon the earth. In fact, it will play a huge role in the building of the New Jerusalem and in the cleansing of the earth. There will be springs of Living Water coming forth from the ground and cleansing that area as well as other places. Living Water as it is talked about in the scriptures is also representative of the cleansing power of the Atonement.

I am not at liberty to discuss this topic any further at this time, however I am confident in saying that for those who have a genuine interest in this topic, the answers can be found in the scriptures.

Through thoughtful study and prayer, people can learn of these things for themselves through the power of the Holy Ghost. Those who are ready to learn more about Living Water will be able to find the answers they seek.

The same form of study pertains to the subject of the Tree of Life. In the Book of Mormon and other scriptures we learn a bit about this tree. I was shown that in the New Jerusalem there will be an actual Tree of Life. It will be located next to the magnificent temple in the center of the city.

The Return of the Ten Tribes

In the Doctrine and Covenants the Lord describes the journey of the Lost Ten Tribes to the New Jerusalem: "And they who are in the north countries shall come in remembrance before the Lord; and their prophets shall hear his voice, and shall no longer stay themselves; and they shall smite the rocks, and the ice shall flow down at their presence.

"And an highway shall be cast up in the midst of the great deep. And their enemies shall become a prey unto them. And in the barren deserts there shall come forth pools of living water; and the parched ground shall no longer be a thirsty land. And they shall bring forth their rich treasures unto the children of Ephraim, my servants.

"And the boundaries of the everlasting hills shall tremble at their presence. And there shall they fall down and be crowned with glory, even in Zion, by the hands of the servants of the Lord, even the children of Ephraim. And they shall be filled with songs of everlasting joy." (D&C 133:26-33)

President Charles W. Penrose commented on the above scriptures by saying: "This indicates the coming of a body of these Israelites, with prophets at their head, from regions of ice and rocks, under divine direction, to receive blessings on this land where are the 'everlasting hills,' and the gathering place for Israel and the keys of power and authority in the hand of the 'children of Ephraim.'

"It is evident, also, that they have important records, containing accounts of the dealings of the Lord with them, and his word concerning them, which they are to bring with them, that they may be joined with the record of the Jews—the Bible—and the record of the Nephites—the Book of Mormon." (*The Improvement Era*, October, 1910, pp. 1087-1088)

I give my additional witness as well. I have seen that these very things will come to pass. I have seen that the day will come when many of the great mysteries of God will be unveiled and the Lost Tribes will be gathered together to feast upon the words of Christ. I have seen that many of our brothers and sisters from foreign lands will bring records with them, and they will serve as additional witnesses of eternal truths.

Elder James E. Talmage gave this warning in the 1916 General Conference: "There is a tendency among men to explain away what they don't wish to understand in literal simplicity, and we as Latter-day Saints are not entirely free from the taint of that tendency. Some people explain that prediction (about the Ten Tribes) is to be explained away in this way: 'A gathering is in progress, and has been in progress from the early days of the Church, and thus the Lost Tribes are now being gathered, and we are not to look for the return of any body of people now unknown as to their whereabouts.'

"True, the gathering is in progress, since this is a gathering dispensation, but the prophecy stands that the tribes shall be brought forth from their hiding place bringing their scriptures with them, which scriptures shall become one with the scriptures of the Jews, the Holy Bible, and with the scriptures of the Nephites, the Book of Mormon, and with the scriptures of the Latter-day Saints as embodied in the volumes of modern revelation." (*Conference Report*, April, 1916, p. 130)

Elder Orson Pratt said the Ten Tribes would come after the building of the New Jerusalem: "After Zion is built in Jackson County, and after the Temple is built the ten tribes will be heard of, away in the north, a great company, as Jeremiah says, coming down from the northern regions, coming to sing in the height of latter-day Zion. They will come, and the Lord will be before their camp, he will utter his voice before that great army, and he will lead them forth as he led Israel in ancient days. This long chain of Rocky Mountains, that extends from the cold regions of the north away into South America, will feel the power of God, and will tremble before the hosts of Israel as they come. They shall be crowned with glory under the hands of the servants of God living in those days, the children of Ephraim, crowned with certain blessings that pertain to the Priesthood, that they could not receive in their own lands." (*Journal of Discourses*, Vol. 18:68, given on July 25, 1875)

I stand as an additional witness of these truths concerning the return of the Lost Tribes. I have seen them traveling by foot, by boat and by other means. They will come from afar, both from the land north and the land south. I have seen that there will be many who will come together, rejoicing in the goodness of the Lord and in His tender mercies.

I have seen that those who have been lost will be found, and that as prophesied, these good people will rejoice in the Lord's goodness and mercy. The Lord's people will become one in unity and purpose. They will be taught and strengthened in their testimonies of the Living God.

Adam-ondi-Ahman

I discussed Adam-Ondi-Ahman in *A Greater Tomorrow*, but some readers have asked how these events will unfold.

I wish to share some of what has been written by our Church leaders regarding these magnificent events. The Prophet Joseph Smith was shown the location of this great future gathering. In 1838 he recorded in his journal: "In the afternoon I went up the river about half a mile to Wight's Ferry, accompanied by President Rigdon, and my clerk, George W. Robinson, for the purpose of selecting and laying claim to a city plat near said ferry in Daviess

County, which the brethren called 'Spring Hill,' but by the mouth of the Lord it was named Adam-ondi-Ahman, because, said He, it is the place where Adam shall come to visit his people, or the ancient of Days shall sit, as spoken of by Daniel the Prophet." (*History of the Church*, Vol. 3:35, given on May 19, 1838)

President Joseph Fielding Smith once explained that Adam held a great meeting with his righteous descendants in this valley during the last years of his life.

President Smith then added: "Not many years hence there shall be another gathering of high priests and righteous souls in this same valley of Adam-ondi-Ahman. At this gathering Adam, the Ancient of Days, will again be present. There will stand before him those who have held the keys of all dispensations, who shall render up their stewardships to the first Patriarch of the race, who holds the keys of salvation. This shall be a day of judgment and preparation." (*The Way to Perfection*, p. 289, published by the Genealogical Society: Salt Lake City, 1931)

President Smith further said, "This council in the valley of Adam-ondi-Ahman is to be of the greatest importance to this world. At that time there will be a transfer of authority from the usurper and imposter, Lucifer, to the rightful King, Jesus Christ. Judgment will be set and all who have held keys will make their reports and deliver their stewardships, as they shall be required.

"Adam will direct this judgment, and then he will make his report, as the one holding the keys for this earth, to his Superior Officer, Jesus Christ. Our Lord will then assume the reins of government; directions will be given to the Priesthood there assembled. This grand council will be composed not only of those who are faithful who now dwell on this earth, but also of the prophets and apostles of old, who have had directing authority.

"Others may also be there, but if so they will be there by appointment, for this is to be an official council called to attend to the most momentous matters concerning the destiny of the earth." (*The Way to Perfection*, p. 290-291)

President Smith then said: "When this gathering is held, the world will not know of it; the members of the Church at large will not know of it, yet it shall be preparatory to the coming of our Savior Jesus Christ as the Prophet Joseph Smith has said. The world cannot know of it. The Saints cannot know of it—except those who officially shall be called into this council—for it shall precede the coming of the Lord Jesus Christ as a thief in the night, unbeknown to all the world." (*The Way to Perfection*, p. 291)

I add my testimony and witness to the words of these great men. I know their words to be true. I have seen it with my own eyes and the Spirit has born witness to me that these things are true. I have a clear recollection of what I was shown, and it is consistent with the words of the prophets and apostles.

These gatherings are real. They have and will happen as has been prophesied by the Lord's servants. The Lord will continue to prepare his servants, even the prophets, for the great day of His return. He loves us and He is doing all in His power to prepare us for His glorious return.

Father in Heaven fulfills all of His promises to his children. The promises made regarding the gatherings at Adam-Ondi-Ahman are no exception. He will fulfill all of His promises pertaining to this sacred place at the right time and in the right way.

We do not need to worry about how or when or if these things will take place. We need to put our faith and trust in the Lord and focus on the matters at hand. We need to prioritize focusing on the things we do know, and what the Lord has already revealed to us, so that we can be ready for whatever we are called upon to endure.

CHAPTER SEVENTEEN

The Second Coming of the Savior

I testify that the Second Coming of the Savior will happen. I have seen it, and the appointed day will come.

I want to mention a misunderstanding that some people have regarding the Last Days and the return of the Savior. It is the false belief that if we will live the gospel and purify our lives, we can hasten the time of the Lord's coming and help to usher in the glorious Millennium.

While it is important to remember that we need to strive to create a spiritual environment in our homes and communities, it is also important to understand that our actions in no way impact or determine when or how the Lord will return for His Second Coming. The Lord's plan was created long ago and the time of His planned arrival does not and will not change based upon our actions.

The time of Christ's return has already been appointed. As the scriptures teach, no man knoweth the coming of the Son of Man. Not even the angels know exactly when Christ will come again in power and glory. Of course God knows, and He has given us very clear instructions and specific directions on how to know and understand the signs of the times.

Although no man knows for sure when Christ will come, we can become aware that the day is getting closer. We should pay attention to the signs of the times that are all around us as they unfold before our eyes. Even though we do not know the exact date and time, those who are faithful will have a pretty good idea that we are getting close because they will notice and pay attention to the signs all around them.

Those who are paying attention and listening to the Spirit will be able to discern that the day of His coming is soon at hand. They will be given additional light and knowledge pertaining to all things, including many of the mysteries of the Kingdom. For those who have eyes to see, ears to hear, and hearts to feel, they will know that the Lord is coming and has come.

Most People Will Be Blind to the Signs

I was given examples of some of the signs of the times that the Saints would witness. I saw and heard the reactions of other people throughout the earth as they also witnessed some of these events. I remember clearly how some were completely blinded and could not see or hear anything. I saw others who saw and heard but could not comprehend or understand what it was they were experiencing.

I witnessed others who at first did not know but then later came to an understanding of what they were seeing. Some people excused the signs as nothing more than coincidence. Some explained them away, rationalizing that what they were seeing or hearing or feeling could not possibly be true.

Others pretended not to see, hear or feel. Yet the faithful and obedient children of God recognized the signs given them. They recognized the Lord's mighty hand and put their trust in Him. They were not surprised, and they were not afraid. Those who were righteous sought to teach others and to help open the eyes, ears and hearts of those who could not or would not recognize the reality of what was going on around them.

Those who were living in a manner in keeping with the Spirit were given clear direction and understanding as to what was going on and what they needed to do to shield and protect themselves and others. Those who followed the promptings of the Spirit were given increased spiritual and temporal protection through the power of the Priesthood. Those who obeyed the Lord's commandments were prepared for our Savior's return.

The day of the Second Coming of the Lord is fixed and established, just as the day of his First Coming was fixed and established in the beginning before the world was created.

Isaiah, Nephi, Abinadi and other prophets and apostles did not prophesy and call upon people to repent so that Christ could come into mortality sooner. The warnings and prophesies given to us pertaining to our day are not and have not been given so that the Lord will stay His hand or speed up the process. The Second Coming will not be postponed because of wickedness and it will not be hurried by an increase in righteousness.

President Gordon B. Hinckley said, "The God of heaven has ordained that day. The prophets of all dispensations have spoken of it. We know not when it will come, but its dawning is certain." (*Teachings of Gordon B. Hinckley*, 1997, p. 577)

We Must Watch for His Coming

The common understanding is that Christ will come suddenly and unexpectedly when the general population is unprepared, not ready, and not watching. That is true.

It is also true that not even the most faithful Saints of God will know the exact time of the Savior's return. The scriptures teach us that He will come "as a thief in the night." (Joseph Smith-Matthew 1:40; D&C 39:21)

However, this does not need to be the case with us. The Lord has said, "And again, verily I say unto you, the coming of the Lord draweth nigh, and it overtaketh the world as a thief in the night—therefore, gird up your loins, that you may be the children of light, and that day shall not overtake you as a thief." (D&C 106:4-5)

We may not know the specific hour or the day when our Lord will come, but we can know the season of Christ's return. We can know the day is nigh when our Master will come to take His proper seat to rule and reign in the temples of our God and on the earth forever more.

One of the ways that I know this is true is because I have been shown this many times. Although I have rarely been shown or otherwise been given specific dates and times of certain events, I have been shown sequences of events.

I have often been given insight or a "heads up" pertaining to things in my personal life. This is not always the case, but it has happened to me a number of times. A few clear examples of this include foreknowledge given to me before I became pregnant with each of my three children.

Another example is the personal revelation I have been given regarding big changes that have come in my life such as job changes for my husband, moves, and certain events that have had a significant impact on me or my family. I haven't usually known the exact dates, but the Lord has shown me or told me that something will happen in "the Spring," or "in May," or "within a few weeks."

As I have said, we may not be told exact timing, but the Spirit will often tell us the season in which something important may occur. As we do our part to live worthy of the Spirit and we watch, listen and obey, the Lord will let us know that the season of His return is upon us.

Those who "are wise and have received the truth, and have

taken the Holy Spirit for their guide, and have not been deceived" (D&C 45:57) will sense and recognize the nearness of the return of the Lord. Those who pay attention to the signs of the times and do all they can to listen to and obey the promptings of the Spirit will be strengthened, fortified, and prepared for that day.

It is my hope and prayer that we will search the scriptures so that we will each learn to discern the light from the dark. It is my hope that we will each do what is needed to help prepare ourselves, our families and others to receive the Lord at His coming. I pray that we will find within us greater strength and determination to heed the Lord's counsel and to follow the Lord's appointed prophet.

I know that as we do so, we will be blessed in ways we cannot even begin to imagine. I know that as we put our faith and trust in the Lord and in His servants, we will be protected. We will find rest for our weary souls and an increased measure of love, hope and divine guidance.

Through the power of the Atonement, we will come to know without a doubt that the Lord loves us and that He does indeed have a beautiful plan for us. We will be continually reminded that we are not alone on our life's journey. We will have angels round about us to buoy us up and to help us accomplish our individual life's missions.

In the Doctrine & Covenants, the Lord himself says, "And all flesh shall see me together. And every corruptible thing, both of man, or of the beasts of the field, or of the fish of the sea, that dwells upon all the face of the earth, shall be consumed. And also that of element shall melt with fervent heat; and all things shall become new, that my knowledge and glory may dwell upon the earth." (D&C 101:23-25)

Two prophets in Jerusalem

Elder Bruce R. McConkie of the Quorum of the Twelve Apostles wrote the following in his book *The Millennial Messiah* concerning these two prophets:

"The word that comes from the Lord is: 'I will give power unto my two witnesses, and they shall prophesy a thousand two hundred and three score days, clothed in sackcloth.' Who are these witnesses, and when shall they prophesy? 'They are two prophets that are to be raised up to the Jewish nation in the last days, at the time of the restoration, and to prophesy to the Jews after they are gathered and have built the city of Jerusalem in the land of their fathers.' (D&C 77:15)"

He continues, "Their ministry will take place after the latter-day temple has been built in Old Jerusalem, after some of the Jews who dwell there have been converted, and just before Armageddon and the return of the Lord Jesus. How long will they minister in Jerusalem and in the Holy Land? For three and a half years, the precise time spent by the Lord in his ministry to the ancient Jews. The Jews, as an assembled people, will hear again the testimony of legal administrators bearing record that salvation is in Christ and in his gospel. Who will these witnesses be? We do not know, except that they will be followers of Joseph Smith; they will hold the holy Melchizedek Priesthood; they will be members of The Church of Jesus Christ of Latter-day Saints. It is reasonable to suppose, knowing how the Lord has always dealt with his people in all ages, that they will be two members of the Council of the Twelve or of the First Presidency of the Church." (*The Millennial Messiah*, p. 390)

In the Bible, we learn more about their ministry in The Book of Revelation 11:2-12:

"But the court which is without the temple leave out, and measure it not; for it is given unto the Gentiles: and the holy city shall they tread under foot forty [and] two months.

"And I will give [power] unto my two witnesses, and they shall prophesy a thousand two hundred [and] threescore days, clothed in sackcloth.

"These are the two olive trees, and the two candlesticks standing before the God of the earth.

"And if any man will hurt them, fire proceedeth out of their mouth, and devoureth their enemies: and if any man will hurt them, he must in this manner be killed.

"These have power to shut heaven, that it rain not in the days of their prophecy: and have power over waters to turn them to blood, and to smite the earth with all plagues, as often as they will.

"And when they shall have finished their testimony, the beast that ascendeth out of the bottomless pit shall make war against them, and shall overcome them, and kill them.

"And their dead bodies [shall lie] in the street of the great city, which spiritually is called Sodom and Egypt, where also our Lord was crucified.

"And they of the people and kindreds and tongues and nations shall see their dead bodies three days and an half, and shall not suffer their dead bodies to be put in graves.

"And they that dwell upon the earth shall rejoice over them, and make merry, and shall send gifts one to another; because these two prophets tormented them that dwelt on the earth.

"And after three days and an half the Spirit of life from God entered into them, and they stood upon their feet; and great fear fell upon them which saw them.

"And they heard a great voice from heaven saying unto them, Come up hither. And they ascended up to heaven in a cloud; and their enemies beheld them."

I testify that these words are true. I have witnessed that these things will indeed come to pass as prophesied in the scriptures.

These special servants of God have been foreordained to this great mission. The Lord has called them for this purpose and He is preparing them for the important work they are to do.

We need not fear for them and we need not worry about them or what is to come of them. They have been promised great blessings of protection and guidance. They will fulfill their assignments successfully. I was shown that in return for their diligence and obedience, they will receive eternal glory that we cannot now perceive.

The Resurrection

While talking about death and the resurrection, Joseph Smith said the following, "Those who have died in Jesus Christ may expect to enter into all that fruition of joy when they come forth, which they possessed or anticipated here. So plain was the vision, that I actually saw men, before they had ascended from the tomb, as though they were getting up slowly. They took each other by the hand and said to each other, 'My father, my son, my mother, my daughter, my brother, my sister.' And when the voice calls for the dead to arise, suppose I am laid by the side of my father, what would be the first joy of my heart? To meet my father, my mother, my brother, my sister; and when they are by my side, I embrace them and they me." (*Millennial Star*, Vol. xxi, p. 6)

President Brigham Young taught that the resurrection of those who lived in the last days would come under the direction of Joseph Smith.

President Young taught: "If we ask who will stand at the head of the resurrection in this last dispensation, the answer is—Joseph Smith, Junior, the Prophet of God. He is the man who will be resurrected and receive the keys of the resurrection, and he will seal this authority upon others, and they will hunt up their friends and resurrect them when they shall have been officiated for, and bring them up. And we will have revelations to know our forefathers clear back to Father Adam and Mother Eve, and we will enter into the temples of God and officiate for them." (*Journal of Discourses*, Vol. 15:138-139, given on August 24, 1872)

On another occasion Brigham Young said, "Some person holding the keys of the resurrection, having previously passed through that ordeal, will be delegated to resurrect our bodies, and our spirits will be there and prepared to enter into their bodies." (*Journal of Discourses*, Vol. 9:189, given on July 28, 1861)

I share my personal witness of the truth of these words. I know that we have a Savior. I know that Jesus Christ suffered and died for us, and He has atoned for the sins of all mankind.

I know that through the power of the Atonement, Christ was indeed brought back to life. He lives as a resurrected being. He is real. I know this because the Spirit has testified of these things to me countless times.

I also know that because of Christ's atoning sacrifice, we too will be resurrected. I know without a doubt that God lives and that He loves us. I know that Father in Heaven has created a beautiful plan of salvation, redemption, and exaltation for us.

I know that because of this great plan, we can prepare now for a greater tomorrow.

I testify of these things and add my solemn witness to the testimonies of those who have come before me and to those who will come after me that Jesus is the Christ, the Redeemer of the World, The Holy One of Israel. He will one day rule and reign in Majesty here upon the earth.

I love Him. I know Him. I witness in His name that God is over all. I testify in the name of the Holy Messiah that the day will come when every knee will bow and every tongue will confess that Jesus is the Christ.

I testify that the day will come when we will see the Glory of the Lord's face round about us. We will see for ourselves the marks of the nails in His hands and feet and the wound in His side.

We will feel of His great love for us. The veil will be taken from our eyes and we will learn and know for ourselves that the Lord fulfills all of His promises. We will know without a doubt that God has been, is and will forever be victorious.

I know this, I testify of this, and I bear witness that these things are true in the name of our Savior Jesus Christ, Amen.

APPENDIX

The Emotion Code
and The Body Code

During my experience in the Spirit World, I was shown many things pertaining to my personal life mission. It was made very clear to me that upon returning to my body, my health would continue to be poor. I learned that although I would struggle significantly for many years, the Lord would provide help for me along the way.

I was shown specific people who would come into my life to aid in my recovery. I was taught that as time went on, I would eventually meet many others who would play a part in helping to restore my health. I was promised that if I did my part to seek answers and to follow the counsel given to me, my health would gradually improve and one day I would be made whole.

I was promised that I would be healed completely while in the flesh (not as a resurrected being, but as a mortal), and that this healing would come as a result of my faith and obedience to the Lord's commandments, through the power of the Priesthood as well as other means. I was given specific counsel and direction as it pertained to my health. I was told that I would not be alone in my journey.

It was explained to me that although the attacks from the

adversary would be severe, I would be given the help of ministering angels who would intervene on my behalf and who would help me learn and remember the things I was being shown. It was made very clear to me that when the right time came, the Lord would help me to remember what I needed to do to continue moving forward and to know how to discern correctly.

I was instructed that I needed to do all in my power to live worthy of the Lord's Spirit, so that I would have the power and ability to discern truth, recognize that which was of the light, and be able to discern that which was not of the Lord. As mentioned previously, I was shown specific people living on the earth, as well as those on the other side of the veil, who were foreordained to help me on my wellness journey.

Many of those individuals have come into my life the past several years. Some have come into my life very recently. Others will yet come into my life.

I was also told and shown that in the future, I would play a significant role in helping others heal. I was specifically shown some of the miraculous healings that would occur in my life, as well as in the lives of those around me. It was made clear to me that in the future, I was to serve others in various capacities, including using some of the healing gifts the Lord has given us.

On more than one occasion, it was explained to me that part of the work I was to be involved in was helping to open and heal the hearts of God's children. I saw myself, as well as many other people, on both sides of the veil working to accomplish this goal. I remember very clearly what I was shown and the instructions I was given. I was shown an example of one modality the Lord has provided for us to help us heal.

When I awoke from my experience, I very clearly remembered the things I was taught regarding this topic, and specific people I would one day meet. I did not however, specifically remember all of the names of the people I had been shown, nor did I remember or have clear insight as to how to find them. I just remembered that I needed to seek answers and understanding, and that as I did so, when the time was right, the Lord would provide the answers. It was impressed upon my soul the importance of having faith in the Lord and trust in His plan for me.

I was first shown these things September 28, 2004. Over the course of the next several years, I did all in my power to find answers and to try to figure out what exactly was going on with my body. I went to doctor after doctor, in hopes of finding solutions to the problems I was having, and in hopes of finding out who and what it was that I had been shown while in the Spirit World.

For over eight years I struggled, making progress but knowing I still had not found the true answer to my dilemma. During this time, I was continually reminded in dreams and visions that what I had experienced was real, and what I remembered was correct. I remembered that the Lord had told me I was to share my story "in approximately nine earth years." I also remembered I had been promised certain blessings pertaining to this mission, and that as time grew closer, I would know and understand more.

I experienced many dark moments. The adversary was ever vigilant in his continued and ongoing attacks. I suffered mentally, emotionally, spiritually, and physically. There were many times I felt I could go on no longer. I cried out to God in agony, begging Him for mercy and pleading with Him to help me. I pleaded with Him again and again, asking Him to take my pain away. Many times the pain seemed unbearable.

I struggled with depression, remembering the beautiful experiences I had been given while in the Spirit World, longing to be there and pain-free, yet knowing that I had a long life ahead of me. I struggled to know and understand why it was necessary that I suffer so.

I prayed continually, begging to be healed, to be understood, to be heard. I wrestled with what I knew to be true, what I could not deny, and what it was I was to do with the knowledge the Lord had given me, in every regard. I felt lonely. I felt burdened. I felt tired. At times I felt abandoned, but I never lost hope.

I knew then, just as I know now, that God does not abandon us. I knew that although life is not easy, the adversities I had experienced, and those which I would yet experience in my life were part of God's plan for me. I understood that the trials I was enduring were for my good and were preparing me for the days ahead. In the midst of it all, I tried to be grateful. Some days were better than others.

I know the Lord hears and answers our prayers. I know that He answers them at the right time and in the right way. I know this without a doubt. I have witnessed and experienced this in my own life and in the lives of others countless times. He is there. He hears us. He listens. He cares.

One of the greatest blessings in my life came as a direct answer to many heartfelt prayers. It came at just the right time and in the right manner. Finally, after more than eight years of severe suffering, I was given clear and specific answers as to the direction I was to go regarding my health challenges. Over the course of a two-week period, the Lord showed me in a series of six dreams some of what I had been shown previously, as well as more.

In May of 2012, God finally gave me the information I needed to be able to move forward and improve my health. At the end of the first week, I dreamed three straight nights in greater detail about what I had been shown during my NDE. I was reminded of what I had learned, and I was shown the specific doctor who had been called and inspired by God to bring about this great work.

I was shown scenes and details of this man's life and what had led to his career path. I was specifically told that he had been given a sacred calling, and that in part his mission included helping God's children open and heal their hearts. It was made clear to me that this man played an integral part in preparing us for the return of the Savior. He and others like him had been foreordained to the specific mission of helping God's children identify and release negative energies that cause all manner of disease and illness.

At the end of the third night of dreaming, I had been given a great deal of information about this man and his work, but I still did not know his name and I still had no clear understanding of what it was I had been shown. I had been told that what I was seeing was a form of "energy healing," but beyond that, I had no idea of who he was or where to find him. I had never researched energy healing, but I knew a great deal about it from what I had learned during my NDE and what I had been shown in my dreams.

I remembered very clearly that on numerous occasions I had been counseled about the importance of learning how to discern that which was of the light and that which was not of the light. I remembered that while in the Spirit World, I had been shown that there were certain gifts of the Spirit that came from God and others that were not of the Lord.

I knew without a doubt that the adversary can and does imitate anything and everything that is of the light and for our good, and he uses that for his purposes. I remembered that I had been taught that pure energy healing is from God, but that there were those who practiced certain modalities that were not of the light. I had been cautioned a great deal about this, and had been given specific direction and guidance to help me on my journey to enable me to discern the light from the dark.

I was shown, taught, and told that there are many counterfeits for this work, just as Satan has a counterfeit for everything that is good. Satan and those who follow him have great knowledge and their own powers. They are real and they do have great influence in this area, so we must be very careful.

I also know that one of the tools the adversary uses is to cause people to fear and have confusion. The last thing Satan wants is for God's children to find the true, good healing sources that are abundant on the earth and are gifts of the Spirit and gifts from God. Satan wants us to lump everything in as the same thing—especially those things we do not understand and that which we fear.

Satan has many who follow him—both spirits who were cast out of heaven and many who are alive on the earth today. For those who do not know how to find answers to prayer, or who are unable to discern light from dark—he has an absolute heyday. Like any other spiritual gift, be it speaking in tongues, the gift of knowledge and wisdom, and every other gift the Lord has given His children, Satan has an imitation.

Just because they are "imitation" does not mean they do not work. They do. That is one of the reasons Satan is so good at deceiving so many, and why he will continue to be able to deceive even the very elect. He does and will continue to take the very most sacred powers given to man and twist and turn them to benefit his cause, which is to destroy us.

Think of the temple ceremony. He has a counterfeit for that. Think of the priesthood. He has a counterfeit for that. He has a counterfeit for everything. Of course he has a counterfeit for divine "energy healing" as well.

Knowing this, I continued to pray for further light and knowledge. I continued to pray for guidance, direction, and clarity. Over the next five days, I prayed often to understand what direction the Lord would have me go. I asked Him to tell me who the man was, what it was I was seeing, and why I was seeing it. Five nights after having had the first series of dreams, I had a series of dreams again. The dreams from the previous week were repeated in a sequential order, and at the end I was shown more detail.

This was repeated again the next night, and then again a third night in a row. At the end of the third night (which was actually now six nights of dreaming, one week apart from each other), early in the morning just before I awoke, I was specifically given the name of the doctor. I was told that his name is Dr. Bradley Nelson, and that the work I had witnessed was "The Emotion Code and The Body Code."

It was made known to me that I was to research Dr. Nelson and The Emotion Code and The Body Code. I was shown repeatedly that I was to be involved in this work in helping myself, my family, and others heal from illness and disease. It was made clear to me that this work would not only benefit me, but also my ancestors on the other side of the veil. It was made clear to me that this form of energy healing would be used in the tent cities, as well as in the New Jerusalem and into the Millennium.

I immediately began trying to Google the name Dr. Bradley Nelson. Nothing came up. I tried several times to Google the words Emotion Code and The Body Code. Again, nothing worked. I attempted to Google his name and his work several times over the course of the next two and a half months, to no avail. I went to the public library to see if I could learn anything. Again, nothing.

Eventually, I became frustrated and decided that I would just give it a little time, all the while continuing to pray to the Lord that He would lead me to someone or something that would give me further insight and understanding. I did my best to listen to the Spirit and to patiently wait for more knowledge. I read a few good books, came across some helpful information on alternative healthcare, and asked friends and family if they knew anything about this topic.

Summer came to a close, and my children returned to school. I felt impressed to contact one of my close friends Wendy, who I had seen in passing, but had not visited with for several months. We made plans to get together at her house and to visit for a few hours. This was in early August of 2012.

Wendy was one of the few people the Lord had given me permission to share my story with. She had been there from the very beginning, listening and supporting and serving. She had been a strength and support to me for eight years. At one point in time, she had helped me record many of my experiences. I had learned to love and trust her a great deal. I knew she was a woman of faith and virtue, and I knew the Lord had brought us together for a great purpose.

On that beautiful, sunny August day, Wendy and I spent several hours visiting. We laughed, we cried, and we shared. The time came for me to leave to go pick my children up from school. As I stood and gathered my things, Wendy inquired about my health. She asked how I was doing and how I was feeling. I told her honestly. I told Wendy the Lord had told me I needed to seek answers through alternative health care.

I said to her, "I have hit a bit of a road block. I don't really know where to go from here. I know that you are more familiar with what is out there and that you have wanted to learn more about alternative health care. Is there anything that comes to mind right now that may be of help to me?" (At that time I did not tell her anything about the dreams I had about energy healing, Dr. Nelson, or any of his work I had been shown).

I will never forget this. Wendy stopped, paused for a minute before speaking, and then thoughtfully and cautiously said, "Yes. Have you ever heard of Dr. Nelson? Dr. Bradley Nelson? He does the Emotion Code and The Body Code."

I was in awe. I put my purse down and sat back down in my chair. I responded, "Yes, actually I have. Can you tell me more?"

She explained that Dr. Nelson had a book titled *The Emotion Code*. She informed me that he also had a website, and that I could either find his book on his website, or I could buy it off of Amazon. She wrote the name of his website down for me as I rushed off to pick my kids up from school.

The drive to the school was about twenty minutes. I sobbed the whole time. I could not believe what I had just heard and learned. Wendy had once again helped me find the information I was seeking. I was so humbled. I was so overwhelmed and grateful.

I ordered the book that night, then waited patiently for it to arrive. When it finally came, I was extremely anxious and excited to read it. I was ready to move on, and I knew that the time had come for me to learn more. After more than eight years I was given the further light and knowledge I had so diligently sought. The Lord had heard and answered my prayers. I was on the right path.

I won't bore you with the details of the next few years, but I will share with you that I have experienced tremendous growth and healing. I have been privileged to work with several different practitioners. I was led to each one. I have been the recipient of miraculous healing. I continue to learn and heal, and I am forever grateful for the power of this work and the power of the Atonement, which makes it all possible. It is real, and it is of God.

Energy is everywhere. Everything is made of energy. Our thoughts are energy, our words are energy, and our actions are energy.

The words love and gratitude have the highest energy vibrations of any words we think or speak. That which is of the light has high-energy vibration. That which is of the dark has very low-energy vibration. The higher the vibration, the greater the light, and the opposite holds true for that which is not of the light.

Knowledge truly is power. Pure sources of energy are given to us as we seek further light and knowledge. Divine light is pure energy. The Light of Christ is given to each and every person born on the earth. Our light and knowledge increases based on the choices we make and the influences in our lives. This is how it has been since the beginning and how it will be throughout the eternities. It is a truly beautiful plan.

In an effort to help others, I have decided to include this appendix about The Emotion Code and The Body Code. I encourage you to study it out on your own and to seek your own answers regarding what I have shared with you. I want to be very open and honest in letting it be known that I am in no way being compensated by Dr. Nelson or anyone else for including this information in my book.

Dr. Nelson did not ask me to do this. In fact, I went to him seeking permission and approval to include Emotion Code and The Body Code information in this book. No one has asked me to promote this material. I am including this information because the Lord has instructed me to do so. I know that part of my mission in life is to help others heal through this work and to do what I can to spread the message about The Emotion Code and The Body Code.

I have been shown that energy work will be done in tent cities, under the direction of the Lord. It will be just one of the many healing methods used there and on into the Millennium. The Emotion Code and The Body Code have been given to us for our benefit, from our loving Father in Heaven. They are real, and they work. I know this without a doubt. I have personally experienced the healing that comes from participating in this work and I have seen it change lives.

To learn more about the work of Dr. Bradley Nelson and the Emotion Code and The Body Code, please visit **www.bradleynelson.com** and **www.healerslibrary.com**.

You can also learn more about this modality on my website at **www.julieroweprepare.com**.

ABOUT THE AUTHOR

Julie has been married to her husband Jeff for nearly twenty years. They have three beautiful children, Ethan, Spencer, and Aubrianna. She is the second oldest of ten children. She was raised as a military dependent, and has lived in several different places: Utah, Texas, California, Washington state, New Jersey, Hawaii, upstate New York, northern Virginia, Kansas, Arizona, and Heidelberg, Germany.

Julie received her Bachelor of Science degree from Brigham Young University in 1999, and her teaching certificate from the University of Saint Mary in 2010. She works as a certified Emotion Code Practitioner.

She loves camping and recreational activities with her family, and attending her children's athletic events and music concerts. She also enjoys spending time with extended family and friends.

She is an avid reader and loves learning about history, geography, science and a variety of other subjects. One of her favorite things in the whole world is to do family history work. She also enjoys meeting and talking to new people.

Julie has a passion for missionary work and a strong testimony of the importance of spreading the Good Word. She is very grateful for the tender mercies of the Lord, and has been a recipient of many. She is very grateful for the blessing and opportunity she has been given to share her story.

Please visit Julie's website at **www.julieroweprepare.com** to learn more about her books and upcoming speaking engagements and book signings.

OTHER TITLES BY
SPRING CREEK BOOK COMPANY

A Greater Tomorrow
by Julie Rowe

In 2004, Julie Rowe was a happy wife and mother. Then her health took a turn for the worse. While in a weakened state, her spirit left her body and entered the Spirit World. An ancestor named John greeted her and showed her many wonderful places there. He also allowed her to read from the Book of Life, which showed her a panorama of the earth's past, present, and future.

Julie saw the lives of many historical figures, such as Adam and Eve, Enoch, Noah, and Moses. She witnessed the Savior's mortal life, including his crucifixion and resurrection. She also saw the restoration of the Church of Jesus Christ through the prophet Joseph Smith, and the key events that have led to the Church's growth.

Then Julie was shown upcoming world events that will be both tragic and glorious. She saw earthquakes, tsunamis, famines, plagues, and wars, but she also witnessed how the Lord is watching over His people and is preparing places of refuge to protect them from the coming calamities. Julie was filled with joy as she saw the Saints establish the New Jerusalem and other Cities of Light in preparation for the Savior's Second Coming.

Prior to her return, she was told that at a future time she would be expected to tell others about her experience. That time has come.

As you read Julie's experience, your life will be changed as you feel the Lord's love and concern for each of us.

The Standing in Holy Places series
by Chad Daybell

The five-volume *Standing in Holy Places* series paints a vivid picture of exciting prophesied events that still must occur before the Second Coming.

In the near future, Tad and Emma North and their children live in a United States that is growing increasingly wicked. The Norths and their extended family notice that many Latter-day Saints are being deceived by alluring temptations, and they wonder how much longer the Lord will allow American society to continue its downward spiral.

Then comes an invitation from Church leaders for the Saints to gather together. This invitation isn't well-accepted—and is even openly mocked—but those faithful Church members who trust in the Lord soon find themselves accomplishing monumental tasks. Join these humble yet heroic Saints as they embark on a journey to build the New Jerusalem.

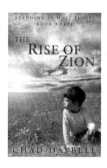

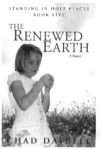

The Times of Turmoil series

Readers who enjoyed Chad Daybell's *Standing in Holy Places* novels will find a new set of futuristic twists and turns in the *Times of Turmoil* series.

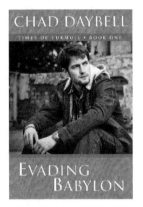

Book One: Evading Babylon

In the near future, natural disasters and economic difficulties have left the United States on the edge of collapse. As faithful Latter-day Saints gather to holy refuges, recently returned LDS missionary Nathan Foster is called to join a secret team to help the Saints find safety. He is expected to devote all of his time and energy to this cause, but he faces a major personal obstacle in doing so—Marie Shaw. However, the deteriorating national situation not only threatens to tear apart their relationship, but puts their lives in peril.

Book Two: Martial Law

After natural disasters and economic difficulties have left the United States on the edge of collapse, the nation's major cities are becoming lawless battlegrounds. Nathan Foster and Marie Shaw find themselves trapped in Chicago, where they must outwit their enemies if they hope to reunite with their families. When the U.S. President makes the crucial decision to allow peacekeepers from the United Nations to help restore order, the nation hopes it will put them back on their feet. Then a major earthquake strikes, and the true intentions of the U.N. forces become more evident.

Watch for **Book Three: Days of Fury** in early 2015!

Other Uplifting Titles

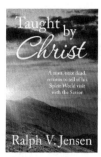

Taught by Christ
by Ralph V. Jensen

Ralph V. Jensen died after suffering a massive heart attack and was given a unique experience while in the Spirit World. He was shown the life and mission of the Savior, with the Savior Himself as his guide. From the Creation, to the Grand Council in Heaven, and finally to the Savior's life, death, and resurrection, Brother Jensen saw it all and shares his experiences in this poignant book.

Through the Window of Life
by Suzanne Freeman

While suffering through a difficult pregnancy, Suzanne Freeman briefly passed away during surgery before returning to mortality. While in the Spirit World she was shown scenes of many future events, including the building of New Jerusalem. Suzanne's message is a fascinating story of the courage Christ's followers will display in the coming years as they prepare for the Savior's millennial reign.

We Lived in Heaven
by Sarah Hinze

This book is a remarkable collection of accounts of families who have had the opportunity to meet the souls of their sons and daughters before they were born. Read about the vivid memories of life in heaven by young children, and dramatic stories of prayers answered by guardian angels who watch over us.

Visit **www.springcreekbooks.com** for more information about these titles, which are available through bookstores, online retailers, and in various eBook formats.